JANICE MARCUCCILLI STROP
JENNIFER CARLSON

MULTIMEDIA TEXT SETS

Changing the Shape of Engagement and Learning

FOREWORD BY P. DAVID PEARSON

CONTRIBUTORS

Holly Dionne
Richard Kuhnen
Stephanie Reid

Portage & Main Press gratefully acknowledges the financial support of the Province of Manitoba through the Department of Culture, Heritage, Tourism & Sport and the Manitoba Book Publishing Tax Credit and the Government of Canada through the Canada Book Fund (CBF) for our publishing activities.

Printed and bound in Canada by Friesens

Cover and interior design by Relish Design Ltd.

Library and Archives Canada Cataloguing in Publication

Strop, Janice Marcuccilli

        Multimedia text sets : changing the shape of engagement and learning / Janice Marcuccilli Strop and Jennifer Carlson.

Includes bibliographical references.

ISBN 978-1-55379-248-2

        1. Language arts (Secondary). 2. Media literacy--Study and teaching (Secondary). I. Carlson, Jennifer II. Title.

LB1631.S77 2010   428.0071'2   C2010-907691-5

PORTAGE & MAIN PRESS

100-318 McDermot Ave.
Winnipeg, MB Canada R3A 0A2
Email: books@portageandmainpress.com
Toll free: 1-800-667-9673
Fax free: 1-866-734-8477
www.pandmpress.com

FSC
www.fsc.org

MIX
Paper from
responsible sources
FSC™ C016245

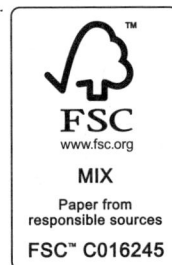

To Mom and Dad, and Bill, John, and Mandy – my anchors and life preservers.
—JMS

To Tait and Claire, who help me remember that dreams do come true.
—JLC

CONTENTS

FOREWORD

In creating *Multimedia Text Sets*, Janice Strop and Jennifer Carlson have given birth to a new kind of book for a new kind of pedagogy for a new kind of reading. Each of these "new" elements is important to this book, and the reader who ventures onto its pages must have a clear sense of "what's new" in this effort in order to appreciate the gift that Janice and Jennifer – and the three teachers (Stephanie, Holly, and Richard) whose stories give life to the effort – have given us.

- If you aspire to be a teacher who helps students become thoughtful, flexible readers – readers who have the metacognitive awareness to change the stances they take toward a text and the tools they use to make sense of it – then this is the book for you.

- If you are a teacher who understands that what we call a *text* varies as a function of our purpose in examining any given artifact we encounter, then this is a book for you.

- If your intuition tells you that the ways in which we position texts in relation to one another matter enormously in how and what students understand from or about a given text, then this is the book for you.

So, what's new about the book? For starters, it is wholly organized around a set of nested metaphors, each of which is important to understanding and appreciating its message. At the most general level, the driving metaphor is the title – *Multimedia Text Sets*. Text is not simply print on a page. Text is any artifact with "semiotic potential," the capacity to prompt us as readers to engage in constructing meaning in response to it – print, art, gesture, movement, sound, even silence.

At the next level down, it is driven by more of a model than a metaphor – Luke and Freebody's Four Resources Model. In fact, the Four Resources Model provides the structure for dividing the book into chapters; there are separate chapters on the reader as decoder, reader as meaning maker, reader as text user, and reader as text critic.

These four labels from Luke and Freebody all refer to "things readers can do to or with a text," so they determine reader stance (what I like to call the *role*) toward a text at any given moment – what Strop and Carlson call *reading practices*. A reader can ask of a text, what does it *say* (that's the decoder), what does it *mean* (the meaning maker), what does it *do* (the user), and *whose interests are served* by its very existence (the critic)?

As if that were not metaphor enough, the authors offer teachers and students a guiding metaphor to help them grasp the essence of each stance. The metaphor for the decoder is the athlete; for the meaning maker, the archaeologist; for the user, the tour guide; and for the critic, the film reviewer. I'm not quite sure about the athlete (I'll elaborate later), but the others work well for me as a reader to focus attention on how each of these resources/stances/roles gets enacted (hence the aptness of the reading practices label) during the reading of any given text (or set of texts). And I can see how teachers could use all four, including the athlete metaphor, to help secondary students understand and enact different ways of "reading" a text. The athlete metaphor is based on analogy between readers and athletes. Athletes, let's say basketball players, learn a few skills, like dribbling, shooting, guarding on defense, a few plays – and then they put them to work in a "game." Readers pick up a few basics about how letters map onto sounds, how text is laid out, how the language of text maps onto the language of talk – and then they put them to work in the "reading game." Neither emerging athletes nor emerging readers wait until they have all the basics mastered before they play their games. That's an important message. So, OK, alright…I do like the athlete metaphor after all.

That's not all that's new about the book. The second, and arguably most important, news in the book is the clear and present voice of the three teachers – Stephanie, Holly, and Richard. Each gives life to the metaphors and the structure of the book by illustrating what Janice and Jennifer's theoretical constructs look like when they come to life in classrooms. I find these accounts of their classroom units particularly compelling, because they are, at once, theoretically grounded and pedagogically engaging; you can actually imagine students enjoying what they are learning. What is remarkable to me is how Stephanie, Holly, and Richard find ways to talk about these constructs with students. I had never thought of explicit – or implicit for that matter – instruction for the Four Resources in the Luke-Freebody model, but here it is! More important, it works – for both teachers and students. I think it works because it gives them a set of tools, and a set of terms, for talking about how to position oneself vis-à-vis the range of texts that students encounter in our multimedia world.

The third "new" thing about the book is its structure. Janice and Jennifer have done a great job of systematically unpacking all of the components in their model in a way that allows readers to come to terms with a complex system. They do it slowly and very analytically, making sure to illustrate each key construct and the complicated ways in which the constructs interact with one another. So we have instructional dispositions – the familiar foci that teachers use to plan and deliver instruction:

- Writing practices
- Discussion across texts
- Vocabulary
- Intertextual connections
- Engagement
- Reading practices

Then we get the five semiotic systems that we encounter in life:

- Linguistic (oral and written; for example, use vocabulary and grammar)
- Visual (still and moving images; for example, use color, vectors, and viewpoint)
- Auditory (music and sound effects; for example, use volume, pitch, and rhythm)
- Gestural (facial expression and body language; for example, use movement, speed, and stillness)
- Spatial (layout and organization of objects and space; for example, use proximity, direction, and position)

Then we get the four literacy practices defined by the Four Resources Model:

- Code breaker
- Meaning maker
- Text user
- Text critic

And then, throughout the book, Janice and Jennifer unpack all three of these ways of organizing one's pedagogical world, so that each scheme is examined in interaction with the other two. So we see writing and discussion as they appear to the code breaker and text user, for example. And we learn how each of the semiotic systems plays out in the instructional dispositions and the four resources. And the amazing thing about it is that it all works. To make this work, to make it manageable for their readers is no mean feat. But the authors manage to pull it off, and in an engaging and highly concrete manner. What's the secret to their success? That's easy – lots of great examples along the way leading to these engaging and detailed scenarios provided by Stephanie, Holly, and Richard.

I haven't said much about the multimedia grounding of the book – the fact that Janice and Jennifer want us to adopt a much broader notion of text than we have used in early generations. And they certainly do (as does one of the teachers, Richard, who teaches a course that focuses on multimedia sources). But from where I sit – and here I reveal my curmudgeonly bias for words on paper (or a computer screen) – that doesn't matter so much. The pedagogical models, the framework they unpack for examining the world of text, the resources/stances, the examples, and the scenarios played out by the teachers, if we took them seriously, would transform our teaching for any and all texts – regardless of whether it was print on a slightly moldy page or hot lava blogging on a social media site. Why? Because the model is theoretically sound and the pedagogy is engaging. Hard to ask for a book that does more than that.

So in the final analysis, I really like this book and recommend it to all those teachers who embrace the idea that our students, more than anything else, need tools to examine text with a critical eye. Our students need an eye toward texts that help them understand why authors write what they do the way they do. In today's very confusing world, students must be able to articulate both the transparent and hidden meanings of the messages they encounter. This book will help you provide your students with the tools they need.

Happy reading! Happy teaching!

P. David Pearson
UC Berkeley
Berkeley, California
December 2010

ACKNOWLEDGMENTS

This book is the result of many voices (texts). First, the thinking and support of the following educators: Mike Ford, Jim Gee, Susan McMahon, Elizabeth Ellsworth, David Pearson, and Kathryn Mitchell Pierce. A special thanks to Annalee Greenberg who first approached us at IRA in Toronto and encouraged us to write this book! Gratitude to Leigh Hambly, our patient editor, for her expertise – this book is the result of her effort and commitment. Our appreciation and respect go to the talented teachers who made this book possible: Holly Dionne, Richard Kuhnen, and Stephanie Reid. We also thank the middle and high-school students who generously and fearlessly approached a new way of learning that they were willing to share.

—Janice Marcuccilli Strop and Jennifer Carlson

I would like to thank my parents, Charles and Frances Marcuccilli, for helping me see and understand the value of stories and the multiple ways of knowing. Thanks to my children, John and Mandy, for keeping me focused on what is important. Thanks to my dear friend Peg Wong for her faith in me. My appreciation goes to my husband, Bill, for his unwavering love and encouragement.

—Janice Marcuccilli Strop

I am so thankful to my children, Tait and Claire, who are inspirations for new ways of thinking and engaging in books. I thank my parents who have always encouraged me to strive for more. And thank you to my husband, Pete, for his extraordinary support, sense of humor, and love.

—Jennifer Carlson

Introduction

It is not enough to simply teach children to read; we have to give them something that will help them make sense of their own lives and encourage them to reach out toward people whose lives are quite different from their own (Paterson 1995, 300–301).

...we can no longer treat literacy ("or language") as the sole, the main, let alone the means for representation and communication. Other modes are there as well (Kress 2003, 35–36).

WHY WE HAVE WRITTEN THIS BOOK

In today's multimedia, multimodal world, messages are no longer limited to spoken and written languages. Many messages are also semiotic and include, among other modes, gestures, images, colors, and music. In the classroom, these (and other) new literacies require a range of practices (Luke and Freebody 1999) that are dynamic and adaptable to a variety of semiotic modes and contexts.

As messages and reading practices continue to evolve, students need to be able to read across multimedia texts and recognize the different perspectives and the rhetorical intent of the texts, authors, and producers. In other words, as students build intertextual connections across texts, they need instruction that (a) is planned and implemented to engage, (b) promotes discussion, and (c) helps them develop reading/ writing practices centered on deep understandings within different text forms.

However, a student's reading ability is not necessarily equal across different text forms and contexts. For example, a successful reader of printed texts is not necessarily a successful reader on the Internet (Reinking and Leu 2007). Thus, teaching students how to read, deconstruct (take apart and analyze), and make intertextual connections across multimedia and multimodal contexts is not only valuable, it is necessary.

In recent years, secondary teachers have expressed a lot of interest in more information on how to plan and teach with multimedia text sets (MTS), primarily because few teachers are trained to teach media or critical literacy (Sullivan 2007). In this book, we will show you the efficacy and benefits of incorporating MTS into your curriculum.

It takes time and planning to incorporate MTS into the classroom. The rewards, however, are well-worth your initial efforts. When you engage your students in MTS, you do the following:

- Expand your teaching to include a variety of text materials

- Incorporate higher-level thinking that teaches students how to read, deconstruct, and make intertextual connections

- Use instructional planning that increases students' comprehension, writing, discussion, vocabulary, engagement, and opportunities to participate in a variety of literacy practices

- Expand perspectives and transcend strategy-based instruction

In *Multimedia Text Sets*, we provide (a) a template to support teachers' efficient use of their time; (b) insight into future planning, processing, teaching, and learning with MTS; and (c) a context within which young people can "make sense" of their lives in relationship to other perspectives.

WHAT MULTIMEDIA TEXT SETS ARE

MTS incorporate many different genres and forms: print, video, music, Internet, photographs, cartoons, and so on. In essence, MTS reflect the texts of today's world. Secondary teachers typically use different genres and forms of texts to support the teaching and learning of content. In our experience, however, teachers do not necessarily teach students *how to read* different text forms. Nor do they *explicitly address* how multimedia texts as a whole interconnect and serve to include multiple perspectives and support deeper understandings of the content and essential concepts (Tomlinson and McTighe 2006). Furthermore, nonprint media rarely are given the same importance and significance as print texts. This lack of attention to other forms of texts ignores the fact that all "texts" – books, ads, film, TV, magazines, music, to name some – are constructed messages. In today's world, an increasingly important aspect of literacy is the understanding that all texts present deliberate, careful constructions. All texts do not just reflect reality but result from the authors' and/or producers' attitudes, perspectives, interpretations, cultures, points of view, purposes, and so on (Alvermann 2001).

One way to increase a student's ability to interpret texts and recognize what is embedded in the texts' messages is to make connections across texts. *Multimedia Text Sets* includes the explicit teaching of how to read different forms and genres of texts and incorporates the following instructional focuses:

- Writing practices

- Discussion across texts

- Vocabulary

- Intertextual connections

- Engagement

- Reading practices

Learning experiences require that we use our knowledge of language (Bruner 1996; Gee 1996; Vygotsky 1978). Reading across texts provides more opportunities to use language to practice literacy skills and strategies and to learn content (Biancarosa and Snow 2004; Hynd and Stahl 1998). High levels of comprehension (increased depth and breadth) are supported as students read critically across multiple texts and text forms (Behrman 2006). Reading across text forms provides engaging opportunities for critical dialogue and advanced comprehension. Thus, collaborative instructional planning that combines text sets and language tools weaves a strong, connective path that supports students' use of strategies and content. It also contributes to a rich context for critical dialogue and advanced comprehension.

How We Define Comprehension

We use the RAND Reading Study Group (RRSG) definition of reading comprehension, which is defined as a process of extracting and constructing meaning. Snow and Sweet (2003) explain that the process of extracting meaning incorporates efficient word recognition and representation of text-based information. Constructing meaning requires building new meanings beyond the text by integrating background knowledge (old meanings) with text-based meanings (new meanings).

RRSG (Ibid.) identifies three interacting elements – reader, text, and activity – that occur within a sociocultural context:

1. Reader: doing comprehending
2. Text: to be comprehended
3. Activity: means for comprehending

In a classroom, the reader's attitude, the specific text, and the assigned task are part of the sociocultural context. The relationships between the three elements are reciprocal – each influences the other.

Advanced comprehension means that students need to read critically; that is, they need to read to figure out "how a text comes to have a particular meaning" (Alvermann and Eakle 2003, 14). Critical comprehension also includes an awareness and understanding of (a) how texts (print, visual, digital) are created; (b) how texts communicate and represent ideas; and (c) how readers and viewers are positioned to respond to the texts in a particular way from a particular viewpoint (Ibid.).

INSIDE *MULTIMEDIA TEXT SETS*

In chapter 1, we introduce the essential components and framework of MTS: text selection, literacy selection, and instructional dispositions. In chapters 2–5, we discuss each of the four roles that teachers and students need to assume in order to become multi-literate. In these four chapters, we visit three middle- and high-school classrooms in which the teachers – Stephanie, Holly, and Richard – have incorporated

MTS into their curriculums. Their units on Americana, the American Dream, and the war in Vietnam provide us with the contexts to illustrate students' inquiry and learning. In chapter 6, Stephanie, Holly, and Richard reflect how MTS have affected the ways they teach. The appendix includes worksheets and chapter summaries that teachers will find helpful for planning their own MTS units.

WHO WE ARE

To introduce ourselves and to help you understand how we came to write this book, we have created literacy dominoes (Gallagher 2004), key events in a chain of dominoes that lead to our current end points.

Janice: Dominoes that lead to my work with MTS:

- In our Dr. Denton's sleepers, my younger brother and I snuggle up in the back seat of our parents' car to watch movies at the drive-in. My parents, especially my father, are great movie lovers.

- My mother reads every chance she gets, while raising four children. She remains a reader all her life.

- The book mobile comes to my neighborhood each week when I am in second grade. I visit the book mobile every week and take home an armful of books to read. Each night, I read by the light of a flashlight under my covers.

- During literature discussions when I am in high school, an English teacher pushes my thinking far beyond my expectations.

- I read to my own children almost from the day each is born. This activity ignites my interest in obtaining a reading degree.

- I listen to my children read aloud our favorite holiday picture books on Christmas Eve and, 25 years later, still hear my voice inflections in theirs.

- My master's degree in reading leads to a position as a K–12 reading specialist. Working with high-school teachers sets in motion my interest in reading to learn.

- I attend a reading-to-learn staff development workshop (CRISS), and I am intrigued enough to become a trainer. I learn to integrate reading/learning strategies across content areas and grade levels.

- My CRISS trainings bring me to the attention of the regional director of instructional programming in southern Wisconsin. She asks me to do a presentation applying learning strategies to video. My first reaction is: "I don't do video. I'm a reading specialist." She is persistent and supportive, so I agree.

- My preparation and presentation of reading/learning strategies with video hooks me into the power of a new kind of visual learning beyond printed text. It also connects me to my life-long love of movies. I spend five years working with instructional programming and become immersed in and engaged by video's learning potential.

- Dissertation research leads me to new literacies that reach far beyond print and video texts and into the high-school classrooms of Richard (an English/media literacy teacher) and Holly (an English teacher and reading/learning coordinator). We begin to build multimedia text sets. We find ourselves (and eventually our students) totally engaged while processing at deep levels from multiple perspectives. We begin to develop MTS with which we teach students the conventions of all text forms. Our students develop high levels of comprehension and engagement as they read across multimedia texts and consider multiple perspectives.

Jennifer: Dominoes that lead to my work with MTS:

- At the end of third grade, my family moves to a new town. I attend a new school and am put into a new reading group: the Turtles. I am upset. In my old school, I was a Robin. Summer school gets me "back on track," but I never forget the experience of being a Turtle.

- I open a Christmas gift. It is the book *Little Women*, by Louisa May Alcott. It has gold-tipped pages and a royal blue ribbon as a book mark. The book is beautiful, and it changes my reading life. I devour everything written by Alcott. This leads me to other woman authors, such as Laura Ingalls Wilder and Lucy Maud Montgomery.

- I begin teaching in a rural school and work to bring the love of reading to my classroom. I implement Sustained Silent Reading (SSR) and encourage the students to bring in any kind of reading material they choose to read. Many students sit on the floor reading magazines, books, letters, short stories. I observe these students in action and had never seen so many seventh-graders quiet and engaged in reading. I receive a stern notice from the eighth-grade English teacher, because I am not making my students read a required novel during SSR time.

- The beginning of my master's degree brings me into a close friendship with my advisor. She shares stories of her own children struggling with reading and what she is doing to support them. I become interested in working with struggling readers, and I begin to think about the kinds of texts that can motivate them and engage them to love texts.

- Dissertation research brings me to a classroom of Title One[1] seventh-grade students, mostly boys, who question why they are in the "stupid" class. From these students, I learn about their interests in reading comic books and skateboard magazines, writing poetry, showing their thinking with art, and their ability to connect their lives with texts – but in a way that traditional teaching does not support. I follow their lead and implement a variety of text types into my teaching.

---

1. U.S. Elementary and Secondary Act that gives funds to schools with a percentage of low-income children who are not performing at grade level in reading and math.

- I am asked to observe an eighth-grade reading teacher in Wisconsin. As I enter her classroom, I am amazed by the tone and atmosphere she has created. The walls are covered with student work and posters. Shelves upon shelves overflow with books. Music is playing. The students are deeply engaged in work and in discussion. The teacher, Stephanie Reid, begins her lesson by playing music to connect the theme of the unit, Americana, to the reading material. I observe the students reading a wide variety of texts. They show their thinking through making art and writing poetry. Stephanie is teaching in a non-traditional way, and it is working. Her students are deeply engaged in text.

- I bring the practices I have seen back to my work with preservice undergraduates and show how art, music, and motion are forms of text. I use well-designed lessons to model ways to implement MTS in the secondary classroom. We discuss, show, view, and describe our thinking behind the text sets and how students and teachers alike will benefit from them.

WHO OUR CONTRIBUTORS ARE

Stephanie Reid hearkens from Rochester, England, where she grew up surrounded by the landscapes and fictional characters of Charles Dickens. She has always loved to read and write, and she pursued this passion by studying English literature at Girton College, Cambridge University. Stephanie received her BA and MA in English Literature from Cambridge University and her postgraduate secondary teaching degree from Oxford University. After teaching English to students in grades 6–12 for three years, Stephanie immigrated to the United States. She and her husband settled in Bayport, Minnesota. She has been teaching in River Falls, Wisconsin, since 2004, first as an eighth-grade reading teacher and then as a language arts/reading teacher. Stephanie is currently working on her MA in Education at Hamline University, St. Paul, Minnesota.

Holly Dionne has been teaching high school for 25 years in Wisconsin, and currently she is an English teacher and reading specialist at Verona Area High School. As a learning resource coordinator, she works with struggling readers and helps shape curriculum and professional development aimed at improving adolescent literacy. Inspired by the promise of genuine student engagement and a new level of meaningful discourse, Holly is building her expertise in helping teachers design MTS across the content areas. Holly is also an adjunct instructor in the reading masters program at Cardinal Stritch University in Milwaukee.

Richard Kuhnen teaches high-school English and media literacy at Verona Area High School. Influenced by the works of Charles Dickens, Kurt Vonnegut, Tom Robbins, Robert Pirsig, Arthur C. Clark, and Mark Twain, he uses a variety of media texts in a wide range of genres to teach reading, writing, and literature. When Richard became enthralled with the idea of information systems and information architecture and the rapidly changing dynamics of "texts" for the 21st century, he began to re-think his practice and to re-envision what literacy in an American public high-school English class could look like. His media literacy courses have grown from one section of 12–15 students to three sections of 26–30 students per class – each semester.

Chapter 1

Essential Components and Frameworks

Literacy as 'the ability to write and read' situates literacy in the individual person, rather than in society. As such it obscures the multiple ways in which literacy interrelates with the workings of power [Gee 1996, 22].

We begin this chapter by using semiotic systems as a planning structure for introducing text selection, because these systems can be used to analyze paper, electronic, and live texts (Anstey and Bull 2006). We then introduce the Four Resources Model of reading, a framework that is used throughout the book. This model is useful for thinking about and planning for the practices that learners engage in for effective literacy (Luke and Freebody 1999; Langer 2002). Following the Four Resources Model, we define and briefly discuss six areas we have identified as the essential instructional dispositions (see page 13) in the planning, development, and implementation of multimedia text sets (MTS): writing practices, discussion across texts, vocabulary, intertextual connections, engagement, and reading practices (see figure 1.1).

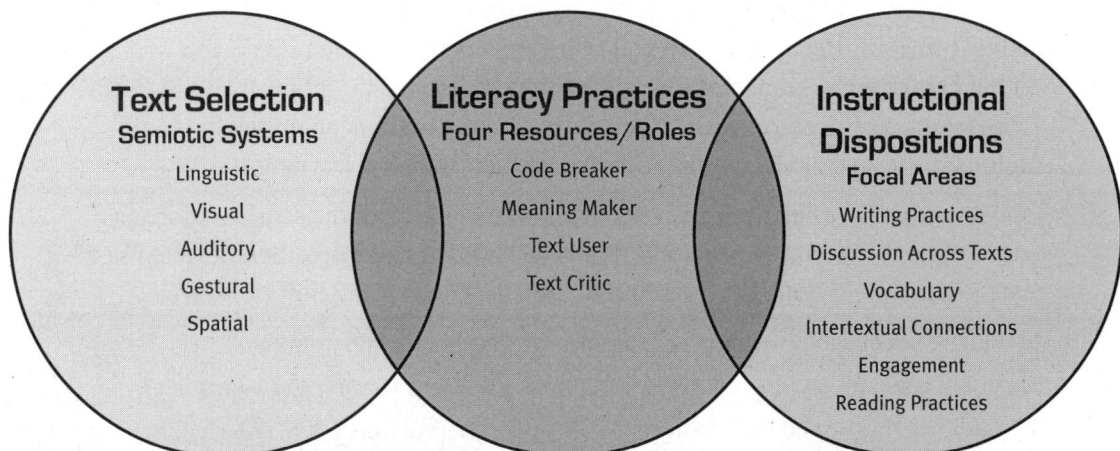

Text Selection
Semiotic Systems
Linguistic
Visual
Auditory
Gestural
Spatial

Literacy Practices
Four Resources/Roles
Code Breaker
Meaning Maker
Text User
Text Critic

Instructional Dispositions
Focal Areas
Writing Practices
Discussion Across Texts
Vocabulary
Intertextual Connections
Engagement
Reading Practices

Figure 1.1 This visual of the Multimedia Text Sets Framework illustrates (left) a structure for balanced text selection, (center) the literacy practices that support learners, and (right) the instructional dispositions that provide a focus for planning, lesson development, and implementation.

The planning of MTS starts with essential concepts, standards-based goals, and assessment plans. MTS provide opportunities for addressing different genres, perspectives, and media. Effective MTS support students' understanding of how different concepts and perspectives intertwine and incorporate teaching methods for deconstructing and analyzing different texts. MTS are designed to bring together ideas in connected paths so students are able to use multiple language threads (Scarborough 2001). This scaffolds students' ability to form high-level understandings and uses the situational interest that results to engage in inquiry (Wilhelm and Smith 2007). This kind of instruction is needed to teach students how to purposefully interact and reflect on multimedia texts in personal and socially significant contexts (Alvermann, Phelps, and Ridgeway 2007; Sullivan 2007; Wilhelm and Smith 2007).

TEXT SELECTION: SEMIOTIC SYSTEMS

In MTS, as in all instruction, the texts selected are critical to the success of student engagement and learning. The texts need to have engaging, provocative content that is both meaningful and immediately accessible. The texts must also allow the reader the opportunity to go deeply into the meaning.

A political cartoon is an example of an engaging, provocative, and accessible text. The reader has to use intertextual connections to deconstruct the literal, surface meanings and dig into the embedded political and social satire. The immediate "I get it!" reaction to the cartoon is engaging, because it is familiar, and, on the surface, the story-line or content is understandable. Upon rereading, though, the text of the cartoon has more depth. This type of text has many layers of meaning, which can be accessed through the literacy practices (see page 9). This process is recursive – the reader moves through the text, circles back, and then asks, "Now what do I think?"

Text that is engaging and accessible promotes students' participation and effort. In MTS, different perspectives and ways that ideas are communicated support students' ability to analyze and make intertextual connections through discussion and writing. As teachers consider content standards, essential questions (Tomlinson and McTighe 2006), and assessments for a unit, they can also begin to think about the kinds of multimedia texts that will engage and support their students' learning.

One way to achieve balanced text selection is to include all of the semiotic systems – sets of signs or symbols (Anstey and Bull 2006, 25) that make up different systems of texts – in each selection. The five semiotic systems (Anstey and Bull 2006) are:

1. Linguistic (oral and written; for example, use vocabulary and grammar)
2. Visual (still and moving images; for example, use color, vectors, and viewpoint)
3. Auditory (music and sound effects; for example, use volume, pitch, and rhythm)
4. Gestural (facial expression and body language; for example, use movement, speed, and stillness)

5. Spatial (layout and organization of objects and space; for example, use proximity, direction, and position)

The linguistic semiotic system (oral and written language) has dominated in the academic setting (Ibid.). However, because texts are increasingly multimodal, a literate person today needs to understand both the conventions within each semiotic system and how combinations of semiotic systems work together to convey meaning within and across texts. One way to create a unit that balances literacy practices and semiotic systems is to analyze selected texts in a chart (see figure 1.2).

Text Type	Linguistic (oral/written language)	Visual (still/moving images)	Auditory (music/sound)	Gestural (facial expression/body language)	Spatial (layout/organization of objects in space)
Classic novel	Prose, dialogue, vocabulary, style	Book cover	N/A	N/A	N/A
Classic film	Dialogue, tone, volume, pitch, rate, regionalisms, slang of the era	DVD cover	Sound effects, music	Actors' expressions and movements	Actors' distance from each other ("social bubbles")
Roaring 20s still images	Captions	Photographs of historic, social, and political events of the era	N/A	Expressions and body language of those in photographs	Camera shots and focus; background
Young adult novels	Prose, dialogue, vocabulary, style	Book cover	N/A	N/A	N/A
Modern film	Dialogue, tone, volume, pitch, rate, dialect	DVD cover	Sound effects, music	Actors' expressions and movements	Actors' distance from each other ("social bubbles")
Newspaper article	Captions, headings, paragraphs	Photographs of Fitzgerald	N/A	N/A	Arrangement of print and subject of photographs
Blog entry	Original entries vs. threaded discussion entries	N/A	N/A	N/A	N/A

Adapted from Anstey and Bull 2006

Figure 1.2 Holly used this chart to help her select texts for her unit, *The American Dream*. Using a chart to analyze selected texts is an effective way to create a unit that balances literacy practices and semiotic systems.

In figure 1.2, the teacher (Holly) listed each system in the type row of the planning guide. In the left-hand column, she listed the kinds of multimedia texts she wanted to use for the unit. In the subsequent columns, she identified the various ways the text could fulfill each system. When completing the text selection planning guide, Holly considered the following guided questions:

- What is the most relevant to the audience?

- What will the audience find interesting or exciting?

- What will the audience not have explored before?

As we discuss each of the literacy practices in chapters 2–5, we will explain how to teach the conventions within each of the semiotic systems in the context of specific texts and teaching practices.

LITERACY PRACTICES: FOUR RESOURCES MODEL

Luke and Freebody (1999, 12) propose the Four Resources Model – four reader "roles" representing a set of practices that support learners as they engage in reading and writing. The model incorporates a "family of practices" that shifts the focus from one method of literacy instruction to a set of inclusive practices.

1. Code breaker (code competence): Code breakers recognize and use fundamentals such as the alphabet, sounds in words, spelling, and structural conventions and patterns in all text types to break the code.

2. Meaning maker (semantic competence): Meaning makers actively work to understand the written, visual, and spoken meanings within a text. They use their background knowledge and understanding of genre and text structure to support their meaning constructions.

3. Text user (pragmatic competence): Text users use texts for a purpose or function by understanding how texts are useful in unique contexts for a particular group of people.

4. Text critic (critical competence): Text critics approach texts critically by recognizing that texts are not neutral, and they understand that texts represent perspectives that may empower or silence others' ideas. Text critics also understand how to analyze texts and consider alternate meanings.

The roles and literacy practices in the Four Resources Model are dynamic and fluid: "…they shape and construct different literate repertoires in classrooms" (Ibid.). MTS facilitate and provide an environment for critically engaging in each of these roles, because students analyze across text types and ideologies that focus on a theme or event. Figure 1.3 can be used to compare roles, practices, scaffolds, and the context in relation to MTS (see BLM 1, appendix B).

Luke and Freebody's set of literacy practices helped us understand how the shape of student engagement and learning is changed in MTS inquiry. We are certain that you will come to the same understanding.

Role [description]	Practices [questions]	Scaffolds [literacy]	MTS [context]
Code breaker (coding competence): breaks code of all texts (print, visual, multimodal) going beyond decoding to recognizing and using structural conventions and patterns	• How do I deconstruct this text? How does it work? • What are its patterns and conventions? • How do the sounds and the marks relate, singly, and in combination?	Students are taught to identify and use semiotic systems* to "make sense of marks on the page...gestures...tone" (Anstey and Bull 2006, 44) in order to figure out how texts work.	
Meaning maker (semantic competence): takes part in understanding and composing all texts based on prior knowledge and experiences of other cultural discourses, texts, and meaning systems	• How do the ideas represented in the text string together? • What cultural resources can be used to make meaning? • What are the cultural meanings and possible readings?	Students are taught to bring their schemata and prior knowledge (based on culture, community, and gender) to texts; they also need to be taught to recognize and compare those to different genres, text structures, and schemata in new contexts.	
Text user (pragmatic competence): knows about and acts on the different cultural and social functions of various texts in and out of school (functions shape text structure, tone, purpose, organization)	• How do the users of this text shape its composition? • What do I do with this text, here and now? • What will others do with it? • What are my options and alternatives?	Students are taught to understand that texts are always situated in fields of economic, cultural, and social fields of power. Students are also taught to read contexts of everyday use – to assess how technical features are used in different contexts and power structures.	
Text critic (critical competence): analyzes and changes meaning of texts by acting on the understanding and critiquing different points of view that can silence and influence	• What kind of person with what interests and values, could both write and read this naively and unproblematically? • What is this text trying to do to me? In whose interests? • Which positions, voices, and interests are at play? Which are silent and absent?	Students are taught to second guess the conditions of text production and text reception. Students are also taught to consider preferred and oppositional readings and how texts are constructed and produced to bring about particular responses.	

Adapted from Luke 2000; Luke and Freebody 1999; Anstey and Bull 2006

Figure 1.3 Literacy practices in multimedia text sets. When using this chart, start with the left column, and select the role you intend your students to assume while they are reading (for example, meaning maker). In column two, prompt students with guiding questions (for example, "How do the ideas represented in the text string together?"). Column three identifies scaffolds, which describe what literacy elements are practiced while the student reads from this perspective. In the right-hand column, provide examples from the topic you are studying.

INSTRUCTIONAL DISPOSITIONS

We have identified six focal areas that incorporate instructional dispositions. We believe each instructional deposition is essential in the planning, development, and implementation of MTS. The six instructional dispositions are:

1. Writing practices
2. Discussion across texts

3. Vocabulary

4. Intertextual connections

5. Engagement

6. Reading practices

Writing Practices

If students are to make knowledge their own, they must struggle with details, wrestle with facts, and rework raw information and dimly understood concepts into language they can communicate to someone else. In short, if students are to learn, they must write (Writing Next 2007, 2).

One of our favorite Calvin and Hobbes cartoons is of Calvin convincing Hobbes that he has figured it all out when it comes to the purpose of writing (see figure 1.4). In the real world, great progress in writing, as with any skill, takes great practice. Many students struggle with taking information from their brain and transposing it onto paper. For these students, the key is to offer writing experiences in a variety of formats for a variety of different purposes.

Figure 1.4 If we all had Calvin's mind, imagination, and great vocabulary, figuring out writing would be simple to learn and to teach.

Defining Writing

The Alliance for Excellent Education report, *Writing Next: Effective Strategies to Improve Writing of Adolescents in Middle and High Schools* (2007), focuses on the importance of good writing skills by offering new insights about methods and strategies that will help improve writing instruction for middle- and high-school students.

The report suggests that no single approach to writing will meet the needs of all students. Therefore, it is important that writing practices include the interweaving of a variety of writing experiences, such as strategies, instructional methods, and genre. For example, these techniques may include summarization, collaborative writing, prewriting, inquiry, and writing to learn.

The four literacy practices (see page 9) can be used to support writing practices in the following ways:

Writer as code breaker: The code breaker uses grammar, paragraph structure, and word choice that focus on organization. Graphics, charts, pictures, nonprint media all contribute to the construction of the written message and authorial intent. The code breaker asks questions such as: How do the conventions within this text help me understand mood and tone? Does the layout of this piece reflect its intent? Thus, the code breaker is able to write and communicate in different genres for different purposes.

Writer as meaning maker: The meaning maker understands and composes meaningful texts for particular audiences by writing to accomplish a goal, or writing to inform, instruct, persuade, or respond. The meaning maker asks questions such as: How will I feel as I read this text? What does the audience already know about the subject matter? Is this piece of writing engaging? Thus, the meaning maker is able to construct and design texts intended for a variety of audiences and purposes.

Writer as text user: The text user understands and composes writing for different purposes (communicating, learning, expression, and so on). He or she also considers options and alternatives in text structure for different audiences in different contexts. The text user asks questions such as: What kind of text is this? What is my goal with this piece of writing? Who is the audience? How does this text connect or relate to other texts? Thus, the text user understands how to shape writing by choosing different alternatives to fit different social and academic conditions.

Writer as text critic: The text critic is aware of and able to use writing strategies to develop ideas. He or she critically analyzes written drafts and transforms them while considering the knowledge and point of view represented and not represented in the content. The text critic asks questions such as: Graphically, where do I focus? How does word selection develop argument? Whose perspective or point of view is evident? Thus, the text critic demonstrates an awareness of intertextuality and text design that influences different audiences and interests.

Writing Practices in Multimedia Text Sets

The writing practices students engage in when using MTS promote communication, learning, and expression writing. At the same time, the students document organizational patterns of their thinking, composing, and reflecting, and they create a written track or history of their thought processes.

Writing to communicate: Writing to communicate means writing to accomplish a goal, to inform, to instruct, to persuade, or to respond (Fulwiler and Young 1982). We have found that secondary teachers commonly ask students to do this kind of writing. Often it is in the form of answering a question on an essay test or on a worksheet, or of developing a five-paragraph essay. This type of writing task is done to meet the teacher's demands rather than writing about something (for example, essay, report writing, explanation paper) that connects to real-world experiences (Jeffrey and Prentice 1997).

Writing to learn: Writing to learn means using writing to think through key concepts, and as a tool to make connections between what is read, understood, and thought (Gammill 2006). Students are encouraged to think through new information, analyze, integrate prior knowledge, and connect thinking across multiple texts. Often, writing to learn is in the form of a dialogue journal, reflective essay, exit card, summary, and so on. Thus, synthesizing texts offer students the opportunity to use language to make meaning of new information in light of what they already know about the topic (Armbruster, McCarthey, and Cummins 2005, 71).

Writing to express: This form of writing encourages students to express personal connections (Britton et al. 1975). Writers' notebooks (as defined by Fletcher 1997) have become popular and are uniquely different from journals. A writer's notebook is for documenting ideas that can be used specifically for different kinds of writing. A journal is often used to record reactions or personal responses to texts. MTS offer numerous opportunities for adolescents to read, view, listen, speak, and think across multiple text types. Students can use writers' notebooks and journals to take on the roles of code breaker, meaning maker, text user, and text critic by documenting reactions, both written and sketched. Calkins (1994) believes that this type of writing should be done daily and should include ideas, wonderings, reflections, memories, and brainstorms of ideas.

Examples of Writing Practices in Multimedia Text Sets

If we listed the kinds of writing we do in an average day, the list would include a wide variety of styles and purposes, such as the following:

- Note to slip into daughter's agenda to have a good day
- Grocery list
- Sticky note reminders (for example, interesting book chapters and quotes, call the soccer coach, ask a colleague a scheduling question, lesson plan development for class next week)
- Emails (for example, to a friend asking about dinner next week, to Mom – just checking in, to a colleague dialoguing about an article we are working on, to a student asking questions about classes, interview questions for a colleague)
- Calendar updating for meetings
- Chapter writing
- Revision on an article
- Margin notes while reading

Similarly, when we assign students different types of writing, we are encouraging them to think about their course material in different ways (Vacca, Vacca, and Gove 2000).

Secondary students are not required to do a great deal of writing in their content classrooms. In fact, adolescents spend only about three percent of their time writing pieces that are a paragraph or longer (Armbruster, Lehr, and Osborn 2001).

The National Reading Panel report, *Reading Next* (2004, 18) states: "...effective adolescent literacy programs must include an element that helps students improve their writing skills." Quality intensive writing instruction is not simply about giving more assigned writing to students. What it does mean is giving a clear, purposeful, and connective writing experience that supports the expansion and development of adolescent readers and writers. When students engage in different styles of writing – from summaries, to essays, to narrative writing – they draw on different kinds of information and experience. They reflect on information in diverse ways, "...acquiring different amounts and kinds of knowledge" (Armbruster, Lehr, and Osborn 2001). When students are offered the same opportunity to experience variety and purpose in their writing throughout their content classes, they develop considerable power over their own comprehension.

MTS provide teachers with opportunities to promote multifaceted approaches – visual, auditory, and print – to discuss and to teach readers how to write about text. MTS incorporate writing activities that challenge adolescents to engage in academic content at high levels. For example, while studying a unit about the war in Vietnam, students use graphic organizers to take notes. This enables them to make comparisons across texts. The students also write essays (in which they argue that watching video of an event can be as effective a means of communication as reading text about the same event). In addition, students create, perform, and critique a poem for multiple voices to convince others' opinions about war crimes.

By making purposes visible to students and offering them an array of roles to take on as a writer, they become better at figuring out writing. With practice, they develop into proficient code breakers, meaning makers, text users, and critics of both their own writing and the writings of others.

Discussion Across Texts

In dialogue with equals...children are less likely simply to defer to the authority of the other's viewpoints, more likely to seek some rational way to deal with differing viewpoints and perspectives, and more likely to actually change their own viewpoint for reasons they understand (Gee 2004, 55).

Enter a middle-school classroom before class begins, and what do you see? More important, what do you hear? Young adults in dialogue. If you listen closely, you will probably catch snippets of discussion about the most popular TV shows, after-school and weekend activities, sports events, and drama in the hallway. Tweens, as well as teens, do talking really well. This is a strength that can and should be taken advantage of in a classroom filled with literacy.

Many secondary students look upon reading as "…a passive act of receiving someone else's meaning" (Wilhelm 1995, 13). However, when student readers engage in discussions of what they have read, they begin to view reading as an active integration with text rather than as the passive surrender to text.

Defining Discussion

Discussion can be defined as collaboratively constructing meaning and sharing responses, viewpoints, and opinions of others. Discussion gives students opportunities to broaden their ideas about characters, events, and issues they have been reading about. Discussion also encourages readers to make connections between the text, context, and their own lives (Galda and Graves 2007).

The four literacy practices can be used to direct and promote discussion in the following ways:

Discussion as code breaker: The code breaker recognizes the patterns and conventions across social and academic talk about texts. He or she can discriminate between different kinds of texts and use language to articulate those differences. The code breaker asks questions such as: What are the communication patterns and conventions of this group discussion? How do the patterns and conventions inform my interpretation and understanding of the text? What language systems will I use to best describe my understandings of this text – written, auditory, visual? Thus, the code breaker communicates and expresses thinking through social interactions around different text forms.

Discussion as meaning maker: The meaning maker participates in the meaning-making of texts through social and academic discourse. He or she makes connections across text types, topics, or themes and verbally shares ideas, relationships, and experiences related to the texts. The meaning maker also uses language to clarify understandings and misunderstandings while generating new, communal meanings. The meaning maker asks questions such as: What do I have to say about my experiences in relationship with this text? What are the predictions, inferences I can make with this text? How do my perspectives change after engaging in discussion with others? Thus, the meaning maker participates in dialogue that integrates prior knowledge with new knowledge in order to articulate predictions, inferences, and questions.

Discussion as text user: The text user articulates the different purposes and uses of particular kinds of text. He or she is able to determine how different texts are structured and match text forms to a specific context by asking questions such as: What perspective can I share about how this text can be used? What do I have to say about the structure and design of this text in relationship to other text forms? Thus, for the text user, discussion articulates purpose, usage, and context of text forms.

Discussion as text critic: The text critic articulates purpose and point of view within a particular text and across a set of texts. He or she uses the vocabulary of deconstruction to respond to, argue for/against, and take on opposing viewpoints.

The text critic analyzes texts in order to identify the different points of view that can silence or influence a reader. He or she also critiques the relationships across texts, determines the underlying messages, and questions and challenges the perspectives that are present and not present. The text critic asks questions such as: What do I have to say about the underlying messages in this text? What position will I take in this debate? How will I articulate authors' and producers' perspectives in connection with my own? How do my perspectives change after engaging in discussions with others? Thus, the text critic engages in discussions that accept or defend various perspectives.

Discussion in Multimedia Text Sets

Within a unit of study, discussion establishes an environment where middle-years and secondary students can engage in talk and purposeful social interaction that do the following:

- Increase reading engagement: In her research on peer-led literature discussion groups, Almasi (1995, 340) found that students "...were more substantively engaged during these episodes than in their teacher led counterparts." In other words, peer-led discussions allow students to act on their own responses and questions, rather than answer the teacher's questions.

- Increase likelihood of comprehension: Conversation fosters comprehension acquisition (Ketch 2005) when students are given the opportunity to reflect, form ideas, and articulate tracks in their thinking. When teachers and students work together to identify big ideas, talk through concepts, and use effective literacy practices, students become more engaged and metacognitive.

- Clarify confusion when struggling with challenging texts: Gallagher (2004) reminds us that giving students an opportunity for group discussion prompts them to confront their confusion by asking and answering questions, clarifying, thinking beyond the written page, making connections, and encouraging creative approaches to learning. As students become familiar with other learners' perspectives, these opportunities have significant influence on the degree to which they come to understand complex ideas (Keene and Zimmermann 2007, 25).

- Encourage shared responsibility for learning: Peer-led discussion groups can increase and encourage a shared responsibility for learning. This reciprocity occurs when the verbal and gestural reactions of individuals are influenced by one another as they interpret the text (Gall and Gall 1993; Gambrell and Almasi 1996, 25).

Interpretations of the reader, viewer, and listener are not fixed. Rather, interpretations are continually shaped by transactions between experiences and new information (Gambrell and Almasi 1996). Students can, therefore, interact in an interpretive community where various viewpoints are shared and encouraged.

Teachers who use young adult dialogue in middle-school and high-school classrooms can make even the most passive reader and active text participant do what young adults do really well – talk.

Vocabulary

...for instruction of specific words to make an impact on reading comprehension, the understanding must be beyond a superficial level (Irvin et al. 2007, 116).

Most students can walk the walk, but can they talk the talk? In our teaching careers, we have witnessed many students engage themselves in "fake reading" (Tovani 2000). These students spend a lot of time staring at the page and making all of the motions needed to look like serious readers, but, alas, they are just faking. Such students are not even walking the walk! They do not realize that during discussion or writing, they will be unable to talk the talk – the language of the text and author will be missing from their vocabulary. Most middle-school and high-school teachers will not deny the importance of students learning the vocabulary of their particular content area.

All middle-school and high-school content areas have words that support and uphold the subject matter. The technical vocabularies encountered in mathematics, social studies, English, science, art, music, physical education, technology, family and consumer science, and so on can total a lot of words in one day. According to research, most challenging vocabulary words taught in content classrooms are presented to students as lists of vocabulary words for the week (Allen 2007). Even when students are required to write the word definition and use the word correctly in a sentence, most remember/know few of the words.

Gallagher (2003, 21) says: "...students need to take many steps to develop mature vocabulary." They need to read, write, hear, speak, think, view the subject matter, and engage in a variety of experiences around those words. MTS offer a variety of texts from a variety of sources; the language is diverse, yet it is encapsulated within the content.

Defining Vocabulary

Content vocabulary, as defined by Alvermann and Phelps (2004), is the understanding of words and concepts in a particular content area and the ability to apply the words and concepts in accurate and meaningful ways.

The four literacy practices can be used to direct vocabulary instruction in the following ways:

Vocabulary as code breaker: The code breaker decodes language accurately within a particular context, content area, or situation. This includes the ability to speak, write, read, and define vocabulary and incorporates knowledge of prefix, root, and suffix. The code breaker asks questions such as: What is the definition of this word in this context? What other words have the same prefix or suffix? Thus, the code breaker recognizes and uses the conventions of language.

Vocabulary as meaning maker: The meaning maker recognizes the variations in language across contexts and makes appropriate word choices to communicate intent, audience, and content. This includes recognizing the relationship of vocabulary across a collection of texts or in the integration of content areas. The meaning maker asks questions such as: How do meanings change in different contexts and text forms? How does the language of this text communicate the author's intent? What words in the text foreshadow upcoming events? What are the characters feeling? How do I know? Thus, the meaning maker understands the vocabulary enough to comprehend and write a wide range of genre.

Vocabulary as text user: The text user applies background knowledge and social, historical, and cultural experiences to organize, comprehend, verbalize, and compose appropriate texts in the appropriate settings. He or she uses knowledge of vocabulary and knowledge of how language works to scaffold content knowledge. The text user asks questions such as: If I write a response to this text, what words will I use? In what ways is this text similar in its language use to other texts? What words will I select and use from this text if I dialogue about the subject matter? Thus, the text user understands different purposes and uses of vocabulary for different contexts.

Vocabulary as text critic: The text critic analyzes the ways in which vocabulary is used to influence readers, listeners, and viewers. He or she can use appropriate content vocabulary to respond to, argue for/against, and take a stance on an issue. The text critic critiques the relationships across text sets and uses accurate vocabulary of the content area to articulate what is and what is not said in the text. The text critic asks questions such as: What language does the author use to position himself or herself? What is or is not said in this text, and why? What is fact and what is opinion in this text? What language leads me to this conclusion? Thus, the text critic understands that the language and vocabulary of the subject matter have power to influence the audience.

Vocabulary in Multimedia Text Sets

As mentioned, multimedia texts incorporate many different genres and forms: print, video, music, Internet, photographs, cartoons, and so on. Language that varies from text to text is embedded in these diverse texts. MTS incorporate vocabulary activities in which students engage in reading, writing, listening, viewing, and speaking experiences/practices that will develop a repertoire of in-depth vocabulary. Students need opportunities and models in order to use and combine the Four Resources Model in varying ways. Methods to implement rich language into daily instruction include explaining new words and reading aloud a variety of text types. Graphic organizers – such as webbing and semantic mapping, and sorting and drawing – are methods that support vocabulary growth and internalization. Modeling through think-alouds and showing relationships between vocabulary words by developing graphic organizers help students visualize language.

Good vocabulary instruction encourages and models rich information about words and their uses. Such instruction gives opportunity for frequent and varied interaction in and around words and motivates learners into pursuing independent vocabulary enrichment. Indeed, is not that the goal of teaching? It is this independence with words that will allow adolescent learners to both talk the talk and walk the walk in style.

Intertextual Connections

More intertextuality – more looking across texts and letting one text get you to think about others – allows for more well-developed, more nuanced thinking. It is this complexity of thought that allows kids to find new ways to see, think, and act in the world (Santman 2005, 22).

Encouraging students to make connections as they read, to link one text to another, can be a rewarding experience for the student and the teacher...Making comparisons is a form of higher-level thinking. When students juxtapose texts and look for connections among them, they are using the higher-level thinking skills of analysis and synthesis. They are analyzing texts to find common elements and then they are synthesizing their findings into new constructs. Intertextuality promotes higher-level thinking (King-Shaver 2005, 15–16).

All readers make intertextual connections when they approach any kind of text. When adolescents watch a familiar TV show, they make intertextual connections, such as remembering story lines from previous episodes or problems or funny lines of regular characters. When they read a book that is part of a series, the context of the story and the characters are already familiar (Harry Potter books, for example). The intertextual connections can be so powerful that students recognize and weave nuances and minute details from one text to another that are unexpected or new: students' thinking goes beyond the surface level (King-Shaver 2005).

Explicitly helping students make intertextual connections supports them, as Santman (2005) argues, because it gets students to use one text to help them think about the shades of meaning and different perspectives in another.

Readers also use their knowledge of content and knowledge of the text's structure to make meaning. Thus, the more knowledge a reader has, the more complete his or her understandings. With tenth-grade students, King-Shaver (2005, 9) found that the juxtaposition of texts affects students' comprehension of each text: "Students made comparisons, discovered contradictions, elaborated on previous comments, and raised questions; they analyzed and synthesized information and ideas." King-Shaver (Ibid., 15) believes that teachers need to (a) have a clear purpose when they select paired texts, and (b) help students make connections between texts.

Defining Intertextuality

According to Moon (1999), intertextuality is a way of saying that texts are bound together like a woven fabric. Individual texts are part of the larger fabric of culture reflected in language and writing. Intertextual links help us understand texts that use language conventions, genre, text structure, common motifs, and so on. These links can appear to be neutral, but they have a purpose – to communicate beliefs and values.

The four literacy practices can be used to direct intertextuality in the following ways:

Intertextuality as code breaker: The code breaker recognizes the patterns and conventions across texts and how they create similar meanings or very different meanings in different forms and contexts. The code breaker asks questions such as: What are the patterns and conventions in these texts? How do the words, or visual or auditory elements, connect across texts? Thus, the code breaker recognizes and synthesizes patterns and conventions across text forms and in different situations.

Intertextuality as meaning maker: The meaning maker is aware of how ideas are put together. The meaning maker compares the different readings that are found in other texts about the same content. The meaning maker then asks questions such as: What are the possible readings within and across texts? What cultural, historical, or authorial meanings can be considered in responding across texts? Thus, the meaning maker actively constructs meaning through comparisons of structure and the consideration of different readings and responses across texts in different contexts.

Intertextuality as text user: The text user understands how ideas about the same content across different text forms and how contexts are put together and used. The text user asks questions such as: How do the purposes of these texts affect their composition? How do the options and alternatives change across text forms and contexts? What options and alternatives can I – as the reader, writer, or producer – use? Thus, the text user considers how texts shape the point of view and the way texts are structured and sequenced.

Intertextuality as text critic: The text critic is aware each text represents a different perspective that attempts to influence some ideas while suppressing other ideas. He or she compares and critiques text designs and ideologies. The text critic asks questions such as: What interests and values are present in each text? How does comparing texts help illuminate different or missing perspectives in each? What intertextual connections are used to create meanings within each text? Thus, the text critic assumes that texts are not neutral, and consciously explores the intertextual perspectives within and across texts.

Intertextuality in Multimedia Text Sets

When reading familiar texts, students do not always realize they are making intertextual connections, because those links feel so natural or unexamined. With unfamiliar or challenging texts, intertextual links can support students' meaning making. Since teacher questioning is an important component in prompting students to make or recognize intertextual connections, King-Shaver (2005, 19) suggests the following open-ended journal prompts:

- What other book, story, play, or film is related to this text?

- Are themes or issues that we discussed with other texts in this text?

- Can you think of another character or event that is similar in another text?

- Have you seen or read about the theme or event in another text form? What is similar? What is different?

- How does the medium affect the message?

Intertextual connections across text forms and discourse communities (Gee 1999) provide students with a supportive context for understanding reading and writing practices in discourse communities. Hern, Faust, and Boyd (1998, 224–225) explain that discourse communities are groups such as local churches or schools, lawyers or literary scholars. Within each group, members have certain ways of interacting and share values and beliefs. For example, reading everything written by and about Charles Dickens does not mean you are a literary scholar. However, by reading all of Dickens' books and essays about the author and the context of the novels, you make intertextual connections that bring you much closer to the practices of literary scholars.

Anstey and Bull (2006, 30–31) describe some of the ways producers of texts use the technique of intertextuality: (a) parody the generic structure of another text (for example, write a nonfiction article in the style of a fairy tale); (b) mimic the layout of another type of text (for example, create a website to resemble the page of a popular book); (c) draw from a scene, phrase, or music of another movie (for example, use connections to other fairy tales and nursery rhymes such as in *Shrek* or *Enchanted*); and (d) use a combination of genres, artistic media, and styles to make a hybrid text that requires intertextual knowledge for it to make sense (for example, incorporate print and illustrations in a unique format that makes the reader feel like he or she is watching a film.[1] It is important to remember, however, that intertextual links only work when the audience already has the knowledge and experience to make the links.

Engagement

Learning requires engagement and motivation...when a reader is invested and deeply engaged in an effort to comprehend, there is a most effective application of cognitive and metacognitive comprehension strategies....What motivates students to be engaged is often tied to their interests and to topics of importance to their out-of-school communities [Snow, Griffin, and Burns 2005, 28–29].

Competence may be the reason for engagement. But, maybe it's the other way around. Maybe engagement is the cause of competence. If we think hard about motivating our students, if we devise units that address questions of genuine importance, expand our notions of text, value meaningful textual engagement and textual pleasure, and broaden our notions of competence, our students are sure to profit [Wilhelm and Smith 2007, 242].

Students are engaged when they can connect content to their own experiences. Adolescents actively seek meaning when they are answering their own questions about issues that are important in their worlds. Students become invested when they

---

1. The Caldecott 2007 picture-book winner, *The Invention of Hugo Cabret* by Brian Selznick, uses this technique.

are asked to think about a question such as: Why does the American Dream matter to young adults?

When students are invested, they stay "in the box" while they continue to think about ideas more deeply. MTS provide students with multiple opportunities for engagement. Each text that is explored and compared gives students new ideas and questions to think about.

Defining Engagement

Ogle and Blachowicz (2002, 262) argue that good instruction only happens when students are engaged – motivated to learn. When students are engaged in the classroom, they are willing to consciously use their own background knowledge to learn through reading, writing and discussion (Guthrie and Ozgungor 2002). Engaged students do not stop thinking because time is up. Nor do they text friends during a discussion. Engaged students are focused on answering their own questions about issues that matter to them.

A variety of activities and instructional approaches are motivating, and interested students bring more background and effort to these types of reading/learning tasks (Snow, Griffin, and Burns 2005). When adolescents are not invested in reading/ learning, they avoid reading and/or use the reading/learning strategies they have ineffectively. We, like most educators, have encountered our share of adolescents who admit to avoiding or giving up on reading required texts, to skimming texts without purpose to "get done," or to prematurely coming to conclusions based on insufficient information. Adolescents can simply come to a point where they do not value reading (Alvermann, Phelps, and Ridgeway 2007).

The four literacy practices can be used to direct engagement in the following ways:

Engagement as code breaker: The code breaker participates in decoding and encoding a range of texts. Since students use different forms of text in their out-of-school literacy practices, teaching them to decode alternate text forms is engaging, because they already value these. The code breaker asks questions such as: What type of shot is in this film? What does the shot reveal? Which words, images, or sounds are interesting? What messages do they communicate? Thus, the code breaker uses all types of texts to promote engagement.

Engagement as meaning maker: The meaning maker engages in the reading and writing of a variety of text forms. He or she uses background knowledge and interests both to make personal connections and to find social significance in texts (Wilhelm and Smith 2007). The meaning maker asks questions such as: If I were the protagonist, what would I do in this situation? How does this text connect to my own personal experience? What extra information is in this shot, frame, or picture? Why is the information significant? Thus, the meaning maker thinks about other meanings and possible readings across a variety of texts.

Engagement as text user: The text user engages in and leads his or her own inquiry and discussions. He or she has the background knowledge and enough perspectives from different texts to see the similarities and differences for himself or herself. The text user can scaffold understandings of the cultural or practical uses of texts. The text user asks questions such as: How would this text change if I used the ideas in another context? If I were the author/producer of this text, what title or form would I use? In what ways is this text used like others of its kind? Thus, the text user works to recognize the different options and alternatives available.

Engagement as text critic: The text critic analyzes the ways in which text is used to influence readers, viewers, or listeners. He or she is engaged by critiquing texts as well as by responding to and arguing for or against particular viewpoints. The text critic asks questions such as: What kinds of responses to this text are expected? Which positions, voices, and interests are present? Which positions, voices, and interests are silent and/or absent? Why does an artist or filmmaker include or exclude certain images? Thus, the text critic engages in analyzing, critiquing, and questioning texts from different perspectives.

Engagement in Multimedia Text Sets

In classroom instruction, MTS engage students because the texts do the following:

- Promote student-led inquiry
- Reflect text forms that students find interesting both in and out of school
- Change the classroom atmosphere
- Support students as they learn how to read, deconstruct, and analyze across texts

When students are taught to read, deconstruct, and analyze a variety of text forms in MTS, they are motivated to lead their own inquiry and discussion. They now have enough perspectives from the different texts to see the similarities and differences for themselves. Students can form their own questions and talk about a text's construction and meanings in their own terms, not in terms based on the teacher's agenda. Wilhelm and Smith (2007, 233) explain: "Inquiry is not simply thematic study, but the exploration of a question or issue that drives debate in the disciplines and the world… kids need to find both personal connection and social significance in the units and texts we offer them."

The teacher is not the only informed learner. When nonprint media are used in an English class, for example, students show more interested and feel more confident about their background, because teachers relinquish some of their authority (Sullivan 2007).

Although Sullivan is referring to thematic units that incorporate literature, we believe engagement applies to MTS, too (Bean 2000, 637). Adolescents are much more willing to invest in content-area learning of science, math, history, and so on when thematic units include literature.

We also believe that limiting learning to print texts and viewing learning as reflecting text-based information misses many opportunities to engage and empower diverse groups of students (Wade and Moje 2000, 623). For all students be successful, educators need to look for new kinds of texts to support learning.

If we count only print texts as text, and if we view learning as extracting important information or as individual responses or interpretations of text, then we miss many possibilities for engaging all students in learning in multiple ways from multiple texts. We also risk disenfranchising large groups of students for whom print texts are not paramount, because they hold different social or cultural values. Operating from one perspective means that our pedagogical recommendations remain rooted in finding ways to help students become successful according to certain predefined conceptions of success (Ibid.).

When multiple ways of communicating are allowed, the shape of engagement changes. In classrooms where all text forms are explicitly taught and regarded as valid information, learning is not limited to one perspective, one way of knowing in one type of text.

Reading Practices

There is a crack, a crack in everything. That's how the light gets in (Leonard Cohen, 2008).

A number of years ago I began to see myself less as a literature teacher and more of a literacy teacher. What good is it, I asked myself, if a student of mine can analyze a novel while sitting in my class but is later unable to apply these same interpretive skills to the real world?...the world is a difficult text. I want my students to leave my class...with an increased capacity to read it critically (Gallagher 2004, 168–169).

Adolescents sometimes refuse to view texts with layered meanings or "cracks" that might show them another interpretation. In one of Richard's media literacy classes, students were discussing *Monster* (Myers 1999), a novel with two formats: (1) the main character, Steve, and his journal in jail, and (2) Steve's screenplay of his trial. During a discussion of the novel, one student, Cooper, decided that Steve was guilty and refused to consider another viewpoint. Another student, Janice, offered a different perspective to the students' interpretation of Steve's innocence or guilt: "You don't think that his mother's look could be…," and Cooper's response was "You can tell me, but…he's guilty."

The literacy practices that Luke and Freebody (1999) describe (code breaker, meaning maker, text user, and text critic) are important vehicles that "illuminate the cracks" as students read within and across many different text forms. Literacy practices cultivate classroom discussions that unpack texts from many vantage points. What is more, MTS open up and illuminate the cracks with other interpretations, because multiple texts bring different perspectives into discussions. For example, in an interview, Myers, the author of *Monster*, explains how he wants to show that becoming a criminal does not happen overnight. It occurs in stages, with a succession of choices that can take anyone down a criminal path. That information may have prompted students to consider different shades of meaning in Steve's decisions and the author's intent.

Defining Reading Practices

Multiple text sets, as we have defined them, incorporate literacy activities within which students engage in reading practices that include breaking the code, reading for different meanings, and understanding the uses and purposes of various texts (Ibid.). Adolescents are challenged by texts written in different disciplines and in domains that have unique characteristics (Snow, Griffin, and Burns 2005). Therefore, graphic organizers, reading/viewing guides, and questioning strategies are used to support students' code breaking and meaning making (Alvermann, Phelps, and Ridgeway 2007).

Incorporating all four literacy practices fills an important gap in adolescents' literacy development. Adolescents do come to school with:

> amazing literacy practices that often go unrecognized and are undervalued…
> but…may not be very good text analyzers, critical thinkers, or connection
> makers….for the most part, schools have done a pretty good job creating
> readers who are code breakers and perhaps meaning makers, but we've been less
> successful helping students become text users and text critics. And these roles
> seem particularly crucial as more of us get our knowledge from unregulated
> sources (Brenner, Pearson, and Rief 2007, 270–271).

MTS support reading practices within which students can learn content through exposure to and explicit teaching of different text forms and perspectives – providing the light that promotes in-depth analysis and learning of content.

The four literacy practices can be used to support reading practices in the following ways:

Reading practices as code breaker: The code breaker uses texts of all types (print, visual, and electronic) as a continuous part of reading (decoding and encoding). The code breaker incorporates ongoing experiences with texts that go beyond the usual practices of breaking the code of print or of using other text forms as an "add on" to print. The code breaker asks questions such as: How can these texts be read? What processes or steps can I use as I read to recognize the text codes? What can I do to use context to interpret words or images? Thus, the code breaker incorporates routines that value competence in breaking the code across all text types.

Reading practices as meaning maker: The meaning maker uses tools such as graphic organizers and text frames that support construction of meaning across text types, genres, and codes. The meaning maker asks questions such as: How does this text remind me of another text? How can I use what I know about this text and my prior knowledge to understand it? How does the meaning of the content change in a different type of text? Thus, the meaning maker uses prior knowledge and text forms to understand content in different contexts.

Reading practices as text user: The text user incorporates reading the language, structure, and tone in texts to understand how to use them for different purposes that might persuade or inform the reader. The text user asks questions such as: What do I do with this text? How can I use it for a particular purpose? How would the message change in another text form? How does the time period or context of the text shape its meaning? Thus, the text user analyzes and compares how all texts are shaped by intent and contexts.

Reading practices as text critic: The text critic encompasses the analysis and understanding of text from a critical perspective. He or she learns to second guess the conditions of text production and text response. The text critic asks questions such as: What are the preferred and oppositional readings? What is this text trying to do to me? Whose interests are being served? Which interests are silent? Thus, the text critic expects readers to consider different meanings and perspectives constructed and produced to bring about particular responses.

Reading Practices in Multimedia Text Sets

Although MTS incorporate reading practices that allow learners to engage in activities as text users and text critics, instructional support is needed. Students need help as they read across multiple texts (Ogle and Blachowicz 2002). They have to be taught how to extract meaning from texts and use their prior knowledge to construct meaning as they make comparisons across texts. Using charts to compare ideas across texts and prior-knowledge activities that elicit students' background knowledge are useful. Students can be asked to record and compare viewpoints to help them understand and recognize different perspectives. Prior knowledge is essential for actively processing meaning from text (Pressley 2000). "Comprehension requires transaction between the text and the reader's prior knowledge" (Alvermann, Phelps, and Ridgeway 2007, 191).

Reading within and across multiple texts gives students the opportunity to use evidence from one source and perspective and compare it to another source and perspective.

MTS provide a rich context for synthesis and critical thinking. We can support students by teaching them reading practices that help them learn important skills in today's global world (Burke 2007; Gallagher 2004, 154). Burke (2007) says that students' thinking can move to synthesis when they have an opportunity to explore an event or problem from many perspectives. First, they can read across a variety of texts that offer different points of view. Second, students can put together and compare ideas. Third, to argue their position, they can present their ideas in a new context that requires synthesizing from multiple sources.

Gallagher (2004, 168–169) explains the need for critical thinking skills, such as (a) moving beyond a surface-level understanding of text; (b) making connections between the text and other people, books, films, and real-life incidents; (c) challenging the text; (d) judging the author's purpose; and (e) considering what was said and unsaid. Gallagher (Ibid.) argues for reading practices where critical analysis and intertextuality are embedded in the content "...to give students *more* exposure to a curriculum that, when taught with rigor, provides them with richer opportunities to think critically."

In *Multimedia Text Sets,* we show that by expanding beyond genres to multimedia and multiple perspectives, students are supported in their reading of a variety of texts. Students are then taught to synthesize and critically analyze the content and perspectives in the text set. The multiple perspectives and forms of media in MTS provide a context for reading practices that fosters critical competence (Luke and Freebody 1999) as students read across and against texts.

Instructional Disposition	Code Breaker	Meaning Maker	Text User	Text Critic
Writing Practices	Uses text conventions to write and communicate in different genres and text forms for different purposes	Uses understandings to compose and design meaningful texts for various audiences and purposes	Uses knowledge to understand and shape writing by selecting different alternatives to fit social and academic situations	Uses awareness of writing strategies, intertextuality, and text design to influence different audiences and interest groups
Discussion Across Texts	Participates in social and academic talk to communicate and express thinking about different text forms, patterns, and conventions	Participates in social and academic talk that deliberately integrates prior knowledge with new knowledge to make connections across text types and generate new, communal meanings	Participates in social and academic talk to differentiate and identify the purposes, uses, and contexts of different text forms	Participates in social and academic talk to understand, critique, or debate various perspectives within and across a set of texts
Vocabulary	Recognizes and uses vocabulary within contexts, content areas, or situations	Recognizes variations in language across contexts to understand and compose meaning in a wide range of genres and content areas	Recognizes and uses vocabulary for different purposes and contexts	Recognizes and analyzes the ways that language and vocabulary influence readers, listeners, and viewers
Intertextual Connections	Recognizes and synthesizes patterns and conventions across texts and the different meanings within different forms and contexts	Recognizes and compares the structures, responses, and possible readings across texts in different contexts	Recognizes the construction and shapes of different meanings within and across text forms	Recognizes and assumes that texts are not neutral, and explores the perspectives within and across texts
Engagement	Actively participates in decoding and encoding both familiar and new text forms	Actively participates in reading and writing to make meaning and think about a range of meanings across text forms	Actively participates in using background knowledge to inquire about and use different text forms	Actively participates in analyzing, critiquing, and questioning texts from different perspectives as readers, viewers, or listeners
Reading Practices	Develops identities that incorporate routines that value competence in breaking the code across all text types	Develops identities that include the use of meaning-making tools and prior knowledge to understand content in different contexts	Develops identities that use, analyze, and compare the way texts are shaped by intent and contexts	Develops identities that consider different meanings and perspectives constructed and produced to elicit particular responses

Figure 1.5 This chart illustrates the intersection of literacy practices and instructional dispositions.

Chapter 2
Athlete as Code Breaker

Given the diversity of writing systems and their specific print knowledge and conventions...many students will require explicit introduction to the code. But that introduction needn't be decontextualized (Luke 2000, 454).

Learning the four literacy practices (code breaker, meaning maker, text user, and text critic) need not and should not be decontextualized; students should be taught all text types (Luke 2000). When the roles are taught and practiced in the context of a multimedia text set (MTS), students' thinking and engagement are evident.

The role of code breaker of all texts (print, visual, multimodal) goes beyond decoding, to recognizing and using structural conventions and patterns. A code breaker is a reader who can break the code by making sense of the language or "marks on the page" (Anstey and Bull 2006, 44). He or she can use the semiotic systems in various text forms – such as electronic, using gestures or facial expression, by discussion – to make meaning.

When we introduce students to the role of code breaker, we use the metaphor of *athlete* as code breaker. An experienced athlete comes to a game (authentic context) with a set of skills he or she practices, sometimes in isolation and at other times with teammates. An athlete also comes to the game with a set of "traditions" that helps to bolster self confidence. Traditions of a hockey player, for example, may include taping a hockey stick before every game, tying the left skate first, and/or listening to motivating music. These traditions put the athlete in the frame of mind for game play. In the classroom, traditions help students think about the knowledge, skills, patterns, and contexts of the role of code breaker.

A coach teaches his or her players how to anticipate and visualize the play of the game before it happens. This practice and an understanding of patterns and conventions of play open up the possibility of strategic play that is both proactive and defensive. The combination of visualization, a player's personal traditions, and practice lifts the player to a new level. Players who practice the patterns and conventions together also learn how to work together as a team to bring about the results they seek. Any athlete or coach can tell you that some practice outside of game play is important but not sufficient enough for learning to play the game effectively.

In much the same way as coaches plan play strategies, teachers can plan instruction that shows students the conventions and patterns to support code breaking and teach them in the context of the "game" by incorporating this instruction as it pertains to MTS.

In this chapter, we present some classroom examples of the "game" of playing code breaker within MTS. The code-breaker portions of figure 1.3 and figure 1.5 are reprinted here for you to refer to as you follow the classroom lessons (see figure 2.1 and figure 2.2). These lessons model how to focus students in a way that prepares them to read and engage in the text information. The three teachers – Stephanie, Holly, and Richard – provide examples of independent practice and group efforts in which the athlete/code breaker strategically interacts, and recognizes and synthesizes patterns and conventions across multiple texts.

Instructional Disposition	Code Breaker
Writing Practices	Uses text conventions to write and communicate in different genres and text forms for different purposes
Discussion Across Texts	Participates in social and academic talk to communicate and express thinking about different text forms, patterns, and conventions
Vocabulary	Recognizes and uses vocabulary within contexts, content areas, or situations
Intertextual Connections	Recognizes and synthesizes patterns and conventions across texts and the different meanings within different forms and contexts
Engagement	Actively participates in decoding and encoding both familiar and new text forms
Reading Practices	Develops identities that incorporate routines that value competence in breaking the code across all texts types

© 2010 Strop and Carlson

Figure 2.1 This chart shows the intersection of the instructional dispositions and the literacy practice of code breaking.

Role [description]	Practice [questions]	Scaffold [literacy]	MTS [context]
Code breaker (coding competence): Breaks code of all texts (print, visual, multimodal) going beyond decoding to recognizing and using structural conventions and patterns	• How do I deconstruct this text? How does it work? What are its patterns and conventions? • How do the sounds and the marks relate, singly, and in combination?	Students are taught to identify and use semiotic systems* to "make sense of marks on the page…gestures…tone" (Anstey and Bull 2006, 44) in order to figure out how texts work.	

Adapted from Luke 2000; Luke and Freebody 1999; Anstey and Bull 2006

Figure 2.2 The literacy practice of code breaker in multimedia text sets. The right-hand column can be filled in with examples from the topic being studied.

CODE BREAKER IN PRACTICE

As a code breaker, a student prepares to read the text information by (a) breaking down and organizing its elements, and (b) examining how the information interacts as a whole. This is similar to what an athlete does. For example, during a hockey game a player will break down the play and internally organize the elements of time, space, and player placement in a split second. As a teammate, the player will also examine how and what to do next based on the situation as a whole. Much like the team player, the code breaker strategically interacts, recognizes, and synthesizes patterns and conventions within and across multiple contexts.

The purpose of the lesson plans that follow is to model how the role of code breaker is practiced in different grade levels. Stephanie illustrates how code breaking is practiced with seventh graders during an Americana unit. Holly describes how her high-school students practice code breaking in a modern-literature unit about the American Dream, using F. Scott Fitzgerald's book *The Great Gatsby* as the focal point. Richard's unit focuses on the Vietnam War. His students are in a high-school media literacy class that crosses grade levels and ability levels.

While reading and analyzing each lesson, ask yourself the following questions:

1. How are my students thinking like athletes and code breaking the text?
2. How do I support and encourage students to maintain and effectively use this role in their learning and monitoring?
3. Where will I integrate this role in my own practice?

Stephanie: Americana Unit

Before beginning my Americana reading unit, I facilitate a number of introductory lessons designed to introduce students to the idea that reading is not restricted to the comprehension study of chapter books. I ask students to think about their daily lives and the world around them and to write down everything they read in a typical day. The lists they compile usually total over 200 items, and they soon realize that there is more to being a reader than they previously thought.

Every student needs to become a code breaker if he or she is to be an empowered reader. An empowered reader approaches a wide range of texts with confidence and a game-plan. I also believe that students need to play an active role in code breaking. It is not my place to transmit the methods of reading various texts to my students. Rather, I model how to deconstruct a text, and I provide my students with the opportunity to investigate and build their own methods of code breaking. While I am available to help support and develop students' ideas, I also encourage independence. The lesson sequence that follows marks my students' entry into the world of code breaking – their starting point. The learning that takes place in these lessons provides a foundation upon which we – students, other teachers, and I – can build. As every athlete knows, reaching a goal does not happen instantly. It takes time.

The code-breaking sequence begins with a reminder to students that (a) text is anything that communicates any kind of message, and (b) reading involves the comprehension of a wide range of text types. We then visit the reading lists the students have compiled and discuss some of the more surprising items on the lists.

Previous discussions have focused on dance as a text, haute couture clothing as a text, and body language as a text. Each of these embodies a point of view and a message. As readers, it is our job to work out what is being communicated. It is our job to unpack the decisions that have been made by the author/creator of the text.

Figure 2.3 Page 4 from the manga novel, *Nausicaä of the Valley of the Wind*

Following this introductory discussion, I use a manga novel (see figure 2.3) to model aloud the act of code breaking. I guide my students through the opening pages of the novel by explaining how I am reading and making sense of what I am seeing.

To model code breaking, I do the following:

1. I show students how a manga novel requires me to hold the book differently, and how I read from right to left – not left to right, which is the way of reading English.

2. I discuss the problems I have when I get to the end of each row of pictures (I am still fighting against the right-to-left method of reading!) and need to figure out which frame comes next.

3. I point out how the images contribute to my understanding of what is happening in the story.

4. I explain how often the images provide clues and information that are not in the writing.

5. I look at the size of each picture (the most important action is usually designated by a larger space), the colors used to portray places and characters, and even the costumes and architecture featured in the illustrations. I emphasize that *image is more important in this text than writing*.

6. I model how I resolve my confusion with Japanese vocabulary by referencing either a glossary or the information section at the end of the book.

As I talk, a student scribe records my ideas on the classroom SMART Board. By doing this, my act of code breaking is recorded in writing for students to refer to as they start to work on their own code-breaking tasks.

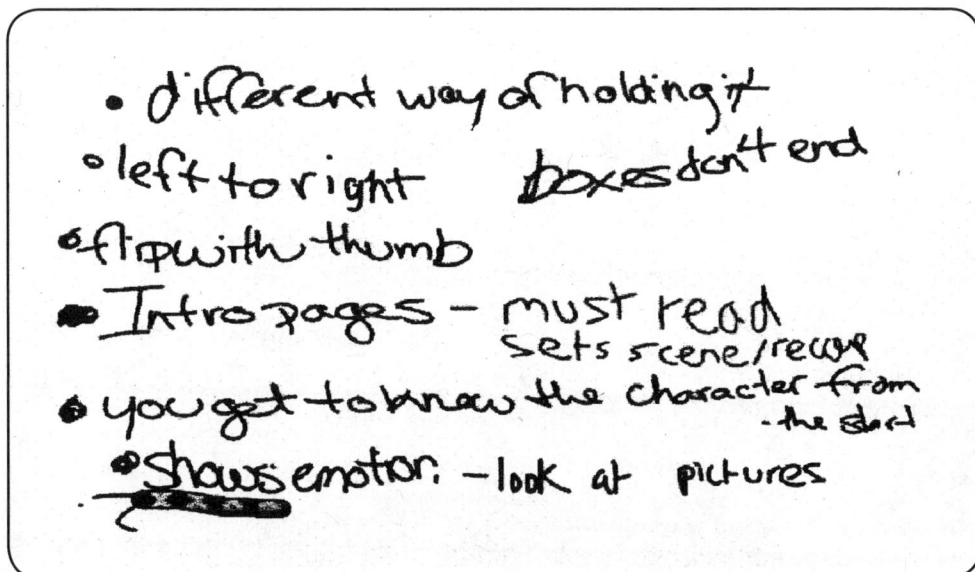

Figure 2.4 A student records Stephanie's code-breaking ideas on the classroom SMART Board.

I then organize my class into pairs of students and allocate a text type to each pair. The text types I use typically include a novel, a magazine article, a poem, lyrics to a song, a music video, a print commercial, a piece of music, a print of a famous painting, a blog entry, a small set of photographs that focuses on people, and a small collection of photographs that focuses on landscapes. All of these text types are genres that students will have access to during the Americana unit.

Next, I ask the student pairs to read the text they have been given and to write down instructions on how to read their text type. Guiding questions are listed below.

- What do you have to do to be able to extract meaning from this text?

- What should you pay attention to?

- Are there any language patterns? Any devices used?

- What is likely to confuse you in this text?

- What should you do if you get stuck?

- How is this text different from/similar to other kinds of texts you have been reading?

I encourage students to pay attention to their thoughts and to not let any ideas escape. Like an athletic coach, my role is to listen to students, help them articulate their ideas, and provide technical advice (vocabulary) that they may need. The writing they do in this initial stage of investigation is a first draft. They will have an opportunity to refine their ideas later.

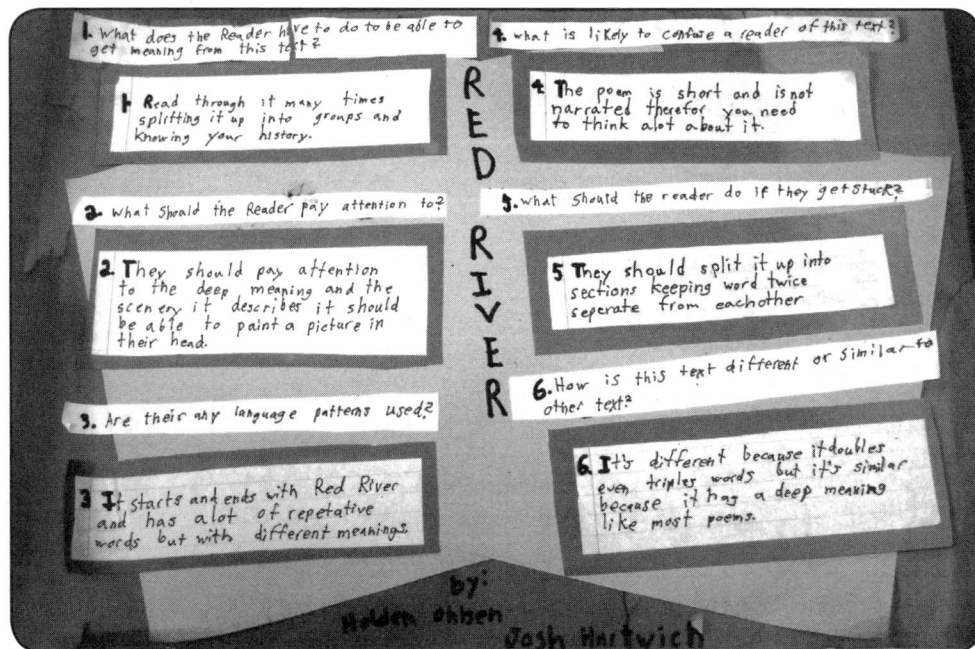

Figure 2.5 Student pairs use guiding questions to write up formal versions of how to read their text type. Students need to remember that they are writing for other students.

Now that the code breaking has started, I ask students to become reading consultants. Each pair teams up with another pair, and the pairs trade the text type they were given and their written instructions on how to read the text. As reading consultants, the student pairs provide feedback on the other pair's ideas by responding to the following questions:

- What ideas do you agree with?

- Do you disagree with anything the other student pair has written?

- Does anything need clarifying or rewriting?

- Do you see something that should have been included?

After both pairs have provided feedback and advice, the groups separate into their original pairs and write up formal versions of how to read their text type. Each pair is allotted one lesson to present its ideas for how to break the code in writing. Pairs can choose their own method of presentation as this encourages them to think through what they have discovered. Students just need to remember that they are writing for other students.

I want my students to learn how to become code breakers, but I also want them to realize that code breaking is similar to an athletic pursuit – it requires ongoing practices that involve flux and experimentation. An athlete does not practice once and become a superstar; he or she faces many different competitors in different environments and must have the confidence to adjust approach and strategy depending upon the circumstance and opposition. Similarly, the written instructions on how to read a variety of texts are used over and over again in future lessons.

Once students understand the role of code breaker, I begin an exploration of what America means to different people. I make sure that a range of text types specific to this theme are available to students. I also make sure that the written instructions are accessible to the students. There will be an opportunity to redraft the written instructions during the main reading segment of the unit, after students have read and studied, in depth, a text of their choice. Students get to choose their text from multiple text sets. When students leave my reading class at the end of the quarter, they know how to deconstruct and comprehend a range of texts. Students remember their role as code breaker and what stepping into this role entails. Code breaking is not a skill that a student encounters once and then has for life. Code breaking takes metacognitive awareness, practice, and patience. The reward is empowerment.

Stephanie's Code-Breaker Lessons

Instructional Disposition	Code Breaker	Teaching Examples	Examples of Students' Work
Writing Practices	Uses text conventions to write and communicate in different genres and text forms for different purposes	I model code breaking while another student scribes ideas on the board. Writing is then discussed and used as an example and reference point for student work.	• Students write to explore and understand a particular text type. • Students write to instruct others in how to read a particular text type. Draft followed by more formal product.
Discussion Across Texts	Participates in social and academic talk to communicate and express thinking about different text forms, patterns, and conventions	I use talk to explain and explore my ideas about how to read a manga text. I listen to students' ideas and suggestions and include them in the ideas recorded on my board.	• Students work in pairs to analyze and explore and understand a particular text type. Together, they draft their "how to read..." instructions. • Each pair teams up with another pair and acts as reading consultants and advisors to each other. Ideas and opinions about each text type are shared.
Vocabulary	Recognizes and uses vocabulary within contexts, content areas, or situations	• During the modeling, I carefully point out things that help me understand the text by explicitly using the correct vocabulary. • I specifically discuss the Japanese words that manga contains and show how I find out their meaning. • I provide a list of useful vocabulary terms to each pair for them to use and get used to.	• Students have access to a vocabulary sheet while they are working on their text type. • Students present their ideas regarding how to read their text type in writing and for an audience. Students encouraged to use relevant vocabulary words.
Intertextual Connections	Recognizes and synthesizes patterns and conventions across texts and the different meanings within different forms and contexts	As I am modeling how to read manga, I compare this text type to other text types. For example, I compare the frames in manga to movie stills, I contrast the back-to-front method of reading manga with the traditional Western way of reading English.	One question that students have to think about is this: How is this text different from/similar to other texts? Students discuss this question in pairs and fours before finalizing an answer in their writing.
Engagement	Actively participates in decoding and encoding both familiar and new text forms	My modeling demonstrates how code breaking is an active process in which the reader has to work and exert effort in order to find meaning.	The code breaking work is largely done by the students. I do not transmit the codes to various texts. My students work to break the code themselves. They do the work. When the students become reading consultants to other pairs, they actively engage in a second text type.
Reading Practices	Develops identities that incorporate routines that value competence in breaking the code across all text types	I discuss the role of code breaker with my students directly, and I provide numerous code-breaking experiences throughout the unit so that students realize code breaking is an ongoing process.	Students take on the role of code breaker and the role of reading consultant/advisor. The role of code breaker will be reprised throughout this unit, and students will be expected to remain conscious of their code-breaking practices.

Figure 2.6 This chart shows how Stephanie integrated all of the instructional dispositions into her code-breaker lessons.

Lesson Aims	Lesson Sequence Details
I want my students to know: • How to become a code breaker and understand what the role entails • What code breaking looks like in action • The kinds of questions that need to be asked in order to take on the role of code breaker • How to deconstruct or decode a text type • Why the role of code breaker is important • The specific vocabulary required to code break different texts	1. I remind students about the brainstorming lists from yesterday, and tell students that today we are going to focus on how we read a variety of texts. 2. I remind students that a text is anything that communicates a message. I give some examples, maybe ideas from yesterday's brainstorm and a *So You Think You Can Dance* or *Project Runway* excerpt. All of these embody a point of view and a message. 3. Our primary job as readers is to act as code breakers. To work out what is being communicated by the author, we have to figure out how to make sense of different texts. We have to unpick the decisions made by an author/creator of a text. It's like origami in reverse. 4. I explain that today and tomorrow's task is to become a specialist code breaker of one kind of text. Students will work in pairs, and each pair will get a certain genre of text. Their job is to crack the code – to work out what the text is trying to say: How would you explain the reading of the text to someone who has never seen anything like it before? 5. I'll model with manga: hold book differently, read from right to left, my problem when I get to the end of the line (want to go back to left-right), how I figure out which frame comes next, how images contribute to my understanding, clues and info the writing does not have, size of pictures, colors used to portray places/characters, costumes, and architecture. Image more important. Japanese vocabulary + glossary. 6. Student scribe records my "how-to-read" ideas on the board as I talk. Did I miss anything? 7. Students get the chance to help me: a "cell-phone manual" page. How do I read this? I really don't get it! What do I need to do to make it make sense? 8. I allocate a text type to each student pair. Pairs are to read the text and write down "how-to-read" ideas. Guiding questions present on the board (see page 38). 9. Pairs work on code breaking their text type. 10. When the majority of pairs are ready, they reveal their reading consultancy roles. Team up with another pair. Purpose: fresh pairs of eyes to look at each text to see if any ideas have been missed. Guiding questions for the consultancy: (a) What ideas do you agree with? (b) Do you disagree with any ideas? (c) Does anything need clarifying or rewriting? (d) Should anything else be included? 11. For the first 8 minutes, students in first pair show the text type they were given and share their "how-to-read" ideas and answers to the guiding questions. The second pair students give feedback and suggest ideas that they think should be included. The process repeats for a second 8 minutes, and the pairs switch roles. 12. Foursomes break back into pairs. Each presents "how-to-read" ideas on a sheet of construction paper. These are copied, laminated, and displayed in room, and are available during Americana unit. They will be used and referred to again, and will also form the basis of a presentation to the rest of the class. Students can use illustrations, diagrams. They can be as creative as possible.

Figure 2.7 Stephanie's code-breaker lesson plans – at a glance

Text Type	Linguistic (oral/written language)	Visual (still/moving images)	Auditory (music/sound)	Gestural (facial expression/body language)	Spatial (layout/organization of objects in space)
Scholastic magazine article	Headline, caption, subheading, written body of article	One large and several small photographs; other artistic details; font details and color	N/A	Present in photographs	Students should pay attention to layout – headlines, quotations, images, frames, and borders.
Song lyrics	Words of the song and language used	Album cover provided with song – contains lyrics, too	N/A	Present in album cover photograph	Presentation of album sleeve can be explored.
Music video	Words of the song and words that appear on screen	Moving image text – technical aspect important here	Music and singer's voice; sound effects	Singer and participants in music video on screen	Artistic design spatially present in the video scenes, shots, editing, and angles
Poem	Language, imagery, word choice	Placement of words and illustrations	N/A	N/A	Form and layout
Young adult novel	Prose, dialogue, speech, word choice, style	Book cover and inside illustrations	N/A	N/A	Placement of illustrations
Blog entry	Written entry	Photographs, images, and color	N/A	N/A	Blog design, sidebars, frames, borders, positioning of information
Photographs	N/A	Photographs of landscapes and people from the *National Geographic* archive	N/A	Expressions and body language of people in the photographs	Camera shots and focus
Print commercial	Slogans, persuasive language devices	Images, art work, colors, font types	N/A	Expressions and body language of people/characters featured in the commercial	Students should pay attention to layout – headlines, quotations, images, frames and borders, etc.
Painting	N/A	Subject/object of painting, technique, colors, style	N/A	Expressions and body language of people in the painting	Composition of the painting

Adapted from Anstey and Bull 2006

Figure 2.8 Stephanie's text selections for her code-breaker lessons

Text Type	Semiotic System	Genre	Learning Purpose	What Students Need to Know	What Students Need to Be Able to Do
Article	Linguistic Visual Gestural Spatial	Nonfiction	Understanding what it means to be a code breaker	• What code breaking looks like • How to deconstruct or decode a text type • Why the role of code breaker is important • Specific vocabulary	• Pay attention to thoughts and ideas • Break a text down into its smallest pieces of meaning • Use relevant vocabulary to identify important text details
Novel	Linguistic Visual Spatial	Fiction	Understanding what it means to be a code breaker	See above	See above
Poem	Linguistic Visual Spatial	Poetry	Understanding what it means to be a code breaker	See above	See above
Blog entry	Linguistic Visual Spatial	Personal writing	Understanding what it means to be a code breaker	See above	See above
Still image	Visual Gestural Spatial	Photograph Painting	Understanding what it means to be a code breaker	See above	See above
Moving image	Linguistic Visual Auditory Gestural Spatial	Music video	Understanding what it means to be a code breaker	See above	See above
Print commercial	Linguistic Visual Gestural Spatial	Persuasive nonfiction	Understanding what it means to be a code breaker	See above	See above

Figure 2.9 Stephanie's text analysis for her code-breaker lesson

Adapted from Anstey and Bull 2006

* * *

Throughout the Americana unit, Stephanie guided students in code breaking challenging texts and guided them to take "advantage of their advantages" by learning to approach a wide range of texts in meaningful ways. She modeled how to deconstruct texts and encouraged students to experiment with different ways of making meaning in different situations. By doing so, her students experienced a variety of texts and took their comprehension to the next level. This was evident in their written work and discussions. Stephanie clearly demonstrates that practice and experience can make the difference in how "the game" is won.

Holly: Gatsby and the American Dream Unit

In modern literature, we have built an MTS that focuses on the American Dream and how the dream has evolved since Jay Gatsby's era. The idea of the American Dream has been around since the Declaration of Independence in 1776, although the term was first coined in 1931 by the writer James Truslow Adams.[1] F. Scott Fitzgerald's *The Great Gatsby* is the cornerstone and the first text for which we adopt the role of code breaker.

We begin with essential questions based on the criteria offered by Wilhelm (2007) in *Engaging Readers and Writers with Inquiry*. Quality essential questions

- Are standards-based

- Require essential disciplinary knowledge to answer

- Are emotive, edgy, and have intellectual "bite"

- Are open-ended

- Are concise and clearly stated

- Are linked to data

- Lead (usually) to new student questions

To move students toward reading across and against different types of media text, we (a) developed three essential questions that emanate from hope, which is the central core of the American Dream, and (b) asked how these texts reveal windows into the American Dream. The three questions are:

1. How has the American Dream changed?
2. What does the American Dream look like?
3. How does the American Dream change in different circumstances?

To stimulate some baseline discussion and reflection, I created an anticipation guide (see figure 2.10) to move the students toward a working definition of the American Dream as it stems from hope.

Our *Gatsby* study begins with a step back in time – back to the Roaring 20s (1920s). When we arrive, we see the blossoming of an increasingly permissive social scene and the post-World War I ennui mushrooming economy. Students need to break the code of the social mores and the promise of wealth that have given rise to the Tom Buchanans, Jay Gatsbys, and Meyer Wolfsheims of Fitzgerald's novel in an era marked by the confines of Prohibition, racism, and sexism.

---

1. Library of Congress http://memory.loc.gov/ammem/ndipedu/lessons/97/dream/thedream/html Retrieved 7/15/2008. In his book, *The Epic of America*, James Adams describes the American Dream as: "…that dream of a land in which life should be better and richer and fuller for everyone, with opportunity for each according to ability or achievement…not a dream of motor cars and high wages…but a dream of social order in which each…shall be able to attain to the fullest…and be recognized by others…."

Anticipation Guide

Directions: *Before* you begin to read the novel, consider the statements in the *left-hand column* (below). In the *second column*, check those statements with which you agree. *While* you are read the novel, consider the same statements from F. Scott Fitzgerald's perspective, and *in the third column* check those with which he might agree. *After* reading the novel, reconsider the same statements, and *in the right-hand column* check those with which you *still* agree.

	Me Before	Fitzgerald During	Me After
1. The American Dream depends mostly on wealth and material prosperity.	____	____	____
2. The American Dream is beyond the grasp of the working poor (like George Wilson).	____	____	____
3. More people would achieve the American Dream if they focused less on financial gain and more on a simple, fulfilling life.	____	____	____
4. The American Dream has faded since the first immigrants arrived in North America to escape persecution and to pursue self-rule.	____	____	____
5. The Civil Rights Era renewed Americans' hope that the American Dream was attainable.	____	____	____
6. Different cultural groups perceive the American Dream differently.	____	____	____
7. Current political platforms are renewing Americans' hope that the American Dream is attainable.	____	____	____

Figure 2.10 Anticipation guides can help engage students in discussion and reflection.

To build background knowledge on the historical context of *The Great Gatsby*, students examine a collection of photos that captures social and political highlights of the years 1919 to 1929. I conceal the captions of the photos, then set out the photos at "stations" around the classroom. In pairs or groups of three, students visit each photo station. At each station, they record notes on "how" they read the photo (their code-breaking process) and write a caption they feel summarizes the main event and impact of each photo.

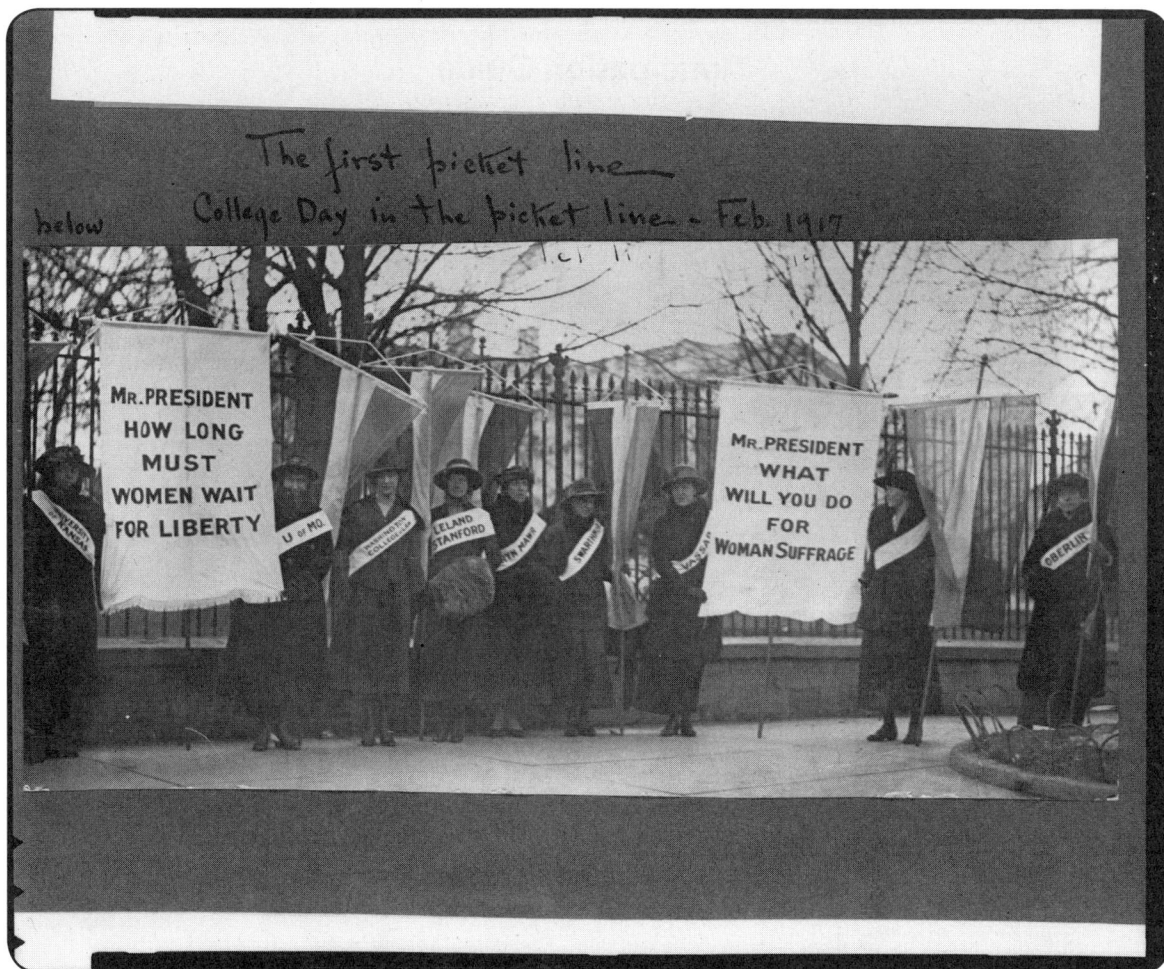

The first picket line —
College Day in the picket line - Feb. 1917

below

MR. PRESIDENT HOW LONG MUST WOMEN WAIT FOR LIBERTY

MR. PRESIDENT WHAT WILL YOU DO FOR WOMAN SUFFRAGE

Courtesy of the Library of Congress, LC-USZ62-31799 (b&w film copy neg.)

Figure 2.11 This is a photograph students examine at one of their photo "stations."

Halfway through this exercise, we reassemble as one large group. On a flip-pad sheet, transparency, or computer-screen projection, we synthesize a list of steps in "how to read a photo." Then, as any athletic coach would do, I have students compare their lists with one another. From this list, we craft a game plan that will help structure the students' practice as they complete the photo-station rotation. Before they resume, however, I unveil the "real" caption on each photo the students have already viewed and written about. I structure this exercise by asking three questions:

1. In what ways are your captions similar to those provided?
2. What do you learn about the Roaring 20s from these captions?
3. What part of this learning is probably significant to our "next game" (reading *The Great Gatsby*)?

Students continue with the exercise, using the class-generated "How to Read a Photo" list and writing captions. Then, we debrief again.

One aspect of any athletic competition is the "lingo" or vernacular of the game. To help students learn some of the slang of Gatsby's time period and to understand the language in Fitzgerald's work, I present students with a vocabulary knowledge rating exercise (Blachowicz 1986). While doing this exercise, students rate their level of vocabulary understanding: "I don't know it," "I've heard it/seen it," or "I know this word, and I can define it." We collate the results informally to determine which terms need to be taught. Each student then works with a partner to research the word meanings, paraphrase the definitions, and create contextually rich sentences. Students share this work by creating a handout that everyone can use as a resource.

When athletes understand what is expected of them during training and competition, their abilities to meet those expectations increase. Likewise, when students are made aware of the style and conventions of Fitzgerald's writing, they are able to break the code. To help focus students' sense of Fitzgerald's language and themes, I introduce them to a quote from his first successful novel, *This Side of Paradise* (1920, 287): "Here was a new generation…a new generation dedicated more than the last to the fear of poverty and the worship of success; grown up to find all gods dead, all wars fought, all faiths in man shaken…."

I model breaking down this quote in the same way a coach would break down a training regimen for an athlete. We discuss what the author intended and how such predictions might impact *The Great Gatsby*.

This discussion is followed by a short exercise in "reading at the word level." Just as athletes must focus on training each muscle to maximize their potential, students must deconstruct Fitzgerald's prose before they can grasp its impact. To establish Nick's attitude about Gatsby's ultimate fate, Nick's attitude toward himself, and Nick's characterization of Gatsby's "extraordinary gift for hope," we examine, as a class, a passage from the first chapter. Students do a writing prompt during our study of chapter 1 or chapter 5 (see figure 2.12) and respond to their peers via the threaded discussion option in Turnitin.com.[2] This exercise returns us to our three essential questions surrounding the American Dream (see above). We create a graphic organizer (see figure 2.13) to help us organize our thinking. It enables students to compare ways that hope determines the American Dream through the perspectives of many literary characters.

---

2. Turnitin.com is an online discussion board that organizes student replies in a way that simulates a "give and take" conversation flow.

TURNITIN.COM THREADED DISCUSSION PROMPTS

Prompt 1

In chapter 1, up to the first hiatus, we get our first impressions of Nick Carraway, the novel's narrator. It is often said that Gatsby is the hero of Fitzgerald's book, but Nick is the central character. Read up to the first hiatus several times, and make note of any new vocabulary (e.g., "riotous excursions").

- What does Nick really think of Gatsby?
- Are these initial impressions or impressions gained from time spent with Gatsby?
- Are we, as readers, led to judge or label Gatsby in any particular way (i.e., favorably, critically, etc.)? Use text support to back up your interpretations.
- Respond to a peer's views. Agree, disagree, extend, embellish, and so forth. Again, use text support!

Prompt 2

In chapter 5, when Gatsby finally meets up with Daisy at Nick's tea party, he takes her on a tour of his mansion. He also has Klipspringer, "the boarder," play piano for them. At the end of the party, as Nick says goodbye to Gatsby and Daisy, his description of Gatsby leaves readers with new impressions of Gatsby. Consider the following paragraph:

> As I went over to say good-bye I saw that the expression of bewilderment had come back to Gatsby's face, as though a faint doubt had occurred to him of his present happiness. Almost five years! There must have been moments even that afternoon when Daisy tumbled short of his dreams - not through her own fault, but because of the colossal vitality of his illusion.

- What does Nick really think of Gatsby?
- How does Nick interpret Gatsby's reactions to Daisy?
- As readers, are we led to judge or label Gatsby in any particular way (i.e., favorably, critically, etc.)? Use text support to back up your interpretations.
- Respond to a peer's views. Agree, disagree, extend, embellish, and so forth. Again, use text support!

Figure 2.12 Thread discussion prompts for *The Great Gatsby*.

American Dream

HOPE

narrow   broad

Individual
Superficial
Immediate

Inclusive
Sustainable
Delayed

Adolescents:
"getting the
girl/boy/partner"

Gatsby & G
"both broad & narrow"

Immigrant & groups outside
mainstream: "opportunity,
hard work"

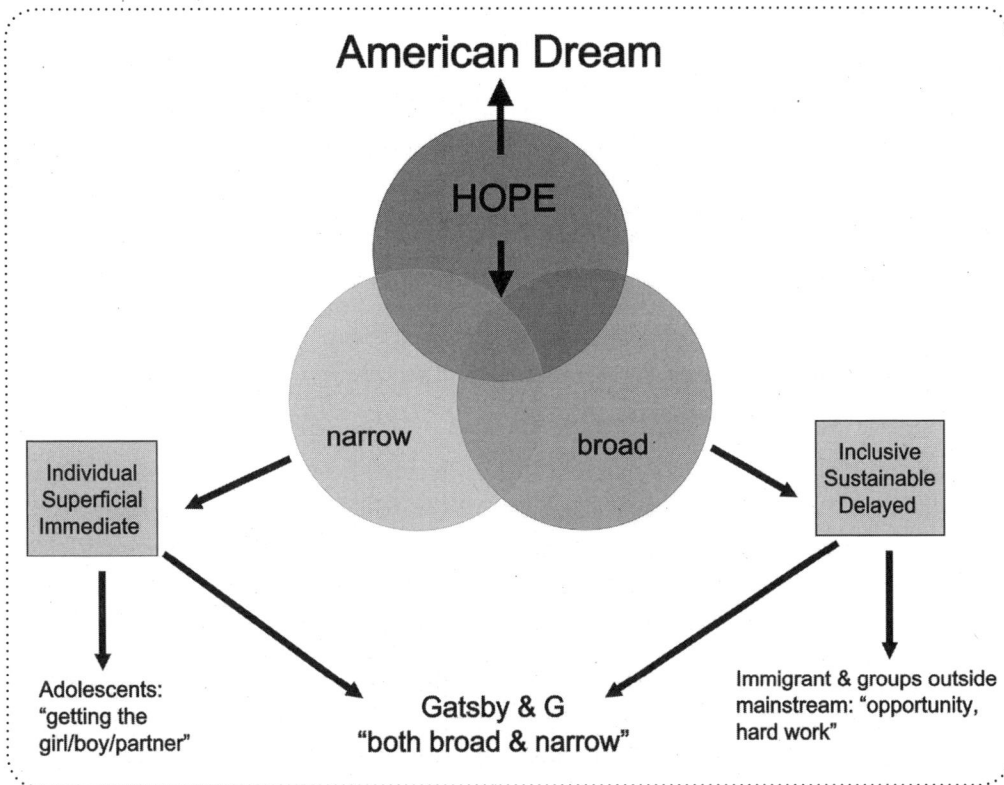

Figure 2.13 This type of graphic organizer helps students organize their thinking.

64,000 Questions

Why did F. Scott Fitzgerald open *The Great Gatsby* with three different parties?

	Chapter 1 Party: Tom & Daisy's	Chapter 2 Party: Tom & Myrtle's	Chapter 3 Party: Jay Gatsby's
Who was in attendence?	Tom, Daisy, Nick, Jordan		
What was the role of each?	Tom was arrogant and took a phone call from his mistress in the middle of dinner. Daisy was flirtatious and warm to Nick, but she hinted that her husband had a cruel edge. Nick was bewildered but charmed by Daisy and Jordan. Jordan was very collected and comfortable being a guest of the rich.		
How? Fitzgerald's language? (Key descriptive phrases or "expansion" vocabulary)	Tom = "supercilious manner," "impression of fractiousness," "paternal contempt" (p.11) Daisy = "unobtrusive [talk with Jordan]" (p. 16), "extemporizing" (p. 19), "cynical" (p. 21) Nick = "hostile levity" (p. 1),"feebl[e]" (p. 21) Jordan = "complete self sufficiency" (p. 13), "polite reciprocal curiosity" & "discontented face" (p. 15)		

Figure 2.14 Students read chapters 1–3 of *The Great Gatsby*, then use this chart to record key information and observe patterns regarding Fitzgerald's intent in opening the novel with three different parties.

Students complete this comprehension guide individually (see figure 2.14), and we discuss their observations as a whole group. Here are some sample student responses reflecting Fitzgerald's purpose in beginning the novel with three parties:

Fitzgerald wants to show the contrasts between the social classes.

Fitzgerald is forcing Nick (the narrator) to choose his new social set.

The author is reflecting the excesses and extremes of the era.

Fitzgerald is showing that people were shallow thrill-seekers.

Fitzgerald believes that money equals power.

Next, I introduce students to a different text or "playing field": the 1974 film *The Great Gatsby*. We watch the first party scene as I model looking at several screen codes: point of view, pacing, dialogue, and music. These codes help answer the question of how this party is unique and what Fitzgerald is establishing at the outset of his novel. Thus, students establish a "baseline" from which to analyze the next two party scenes.

As we watch the scenes of the next two parties, the central question remains: Why does Fitzgerald open *The Great Gatsby* with three very different parties? In pair or small-group discussions, students either change or reinforce their previous viewpoints. Often, they raise new perspectives such as the following:

Fitzgerald is making Gatsby appear mysterious.

Fitzgerald is showing women as weak and flighty, despite their social classes.

Fitzgerald is contrasting the morals and motivations of his main characters.

From this exercise in connecting text, students begin to make predictions on how the author's stylistic choices will inform character development. To facilitate this, I introduce the term *juxtaposition*, and we tie this back to the three party scenes. At this point, students feel they have broken the code. What follows is a "ticket out the door" response to the following question: Other than juxtaposition, what are common stylistic traits of the first three chapters that the film director captures?

Here are some sample student responses:

The author presents scenes as if we were viewing them "live."

Nick Carraway is a first-person narrator who is involved in the action but who may not be honest, even though he claims to be.

Background information on setting and main characters comes in the form of flashbacks.

Fitzgerald uses long descriptive sentences.

Holly's Code-Breaker Lessons

Instructional Disposition	Code Breaker	Teaching Examples	Examples of Students' Work
Writing Practices	Uses text conventions to write and communicate in different genres and text forms for different purposes	I model code breaking for photographs.	• Students record steps for "reading" photographs and generate potential captions. • Students work in small groups to write summary captions for photographs. • Students write to clarify their observations on Fitzgerald's style via Turnitin.com's threaded discussion option.
Discussion Across Texts	Participates in social and academic talk to communicate and express thinking about different text forms, patterns, and conventions	I model deconstruction of opening quote from Fitzgerald's *This Side of Paradise*.	• Students discuss recommendations for steps to read photographs. • They discuss interpretations of Fitzgerald quote as it applies to the era and potentially to *Gatsby*. • Students debrief on photo exercise using three critical questions to tie to *Gatsby*. • Students participate in a threaded discussion on a key passage from chapter 1 or chapter 5.
Vocabulary	Recognizes and uses vocabulary within contexts, content areas, or situations	I introduce students to an exploration of Fitzgerald's style and word choices.	Students compare key elements of first three chapters and create a grid that focuses on Fitzgerald's use of vocabulary that is new to them.
Intertextual Connections	Recognizes and synthesizes patterns and conventions across texts and the different meanings within different forms and contexts	I present strategies of breaking codes and conventions of film by modeling analysis of the *Gatsby* film's first party scene.	Students discuss how the film director's depiction of the scene compares to Fitzgerald's written depiction of the same scene.
Engagement	Actively participates in decoding and encoding both familiar and new text forms	I structure format for students to interpret the film's next two party scenes to establish familiarity with codes and conventions.	The code breaking is initiated by students who share in small groups and discuss further comparisons between the film and novel.
Reading Practices	Develops identities that incorporate routines that value competence in breaking the code across all text types	I model deconstruction and interpretation of sample passage from chapter 1 that reflect Nick's attitude shift through a retrospective, and I highlight Fitzgerald's vocabulary and some characterization techniques.	Students compare key elements of first three chapters and create a grid that focuses on authorial intent and characterization.

Figure 2.15 This chart shows how Holly integrated all of the instructional dispositions into her code-breaker lessons.

Lesson Aims	Lesson Sequence Details
I want my students to know: • How to become a code breaker – what the role entails • What code breaking looks like in action • The kinds of questions they need to ask in order to take on the role of code breaker • How to deconstruct or decode a text type • Why the role of code breaker is important • The specific vocabulary required to code break different texts	1. I introduce the American Dream (AD) with a "centering" discussion exploring its genesis and establishing hope as its core. 2. I have students complete an anticipation guide to register their perceptions for the AD and anticipate perspectives Fitzgerald may offer in *Gatsby*. 3. I have students examine a group of photos from the Roaring 20s and write captions while noting techniques for how to "read" a photograph. Compare these with the "real" captions and compare their "how-to" list with the guidelines from U.S. National Archives. Continue exercise with remaining photos using combined guidelines. 4. Students examine a pivotal quote from Fitzgerald's *This Side of Paradise* to analyze style and potential themes predictive of *Gatsby's* themes. 5. Students deconstruct one of two passages from Gatsby's chapter 1 to focus discussion and compare thinking via a Turnitin.com threaded discussion. 6. Students respond to essential questions by helping create a graphic organizer focusing on the role of hope in building the AD of the literary characters we will encounter. 7. Students read the first three chapters of *Gatsby* and create a grid to compare the *who, what, why*, and *how* of Fitzgerald's portrayal of the three juxtaposed parties. A whole-group discussion follows. 8. I show the first party scene of the 1974 *Gatsby* film and model screen codes to guide students as they analyze the film's next two consecutive party scenes. After viewing these respective scenes, students share and compare the novel and film in pairs or small groups. 9. Students complete a "ticket out the door" to comment on the film director's success at capturing traits common to Fitzgerald's style.

Figure 2.16 Holly's code-breaker lesson plans – at a glance

Text Type	Linguistic (oral/written language)	Visual (still/moving images)	Auditory (music/sound)	Gestural (facial expression/body language)	Spatial (layout/organization of objects in space)
Classic novel	Prose, dialogue, vocabulary, style	Book cover	N/A	N/A	N/A
Film	Dialogue, tone, volume, pitch, rate, regionalisms, slang of the era	DVD cover	Sound effects, music	Actors' expressions and movements	Actors' distance from each other ("social bubbles")
Roaring 20s still images	Captions	Photographs of historic, social, and political events of the era	N/A	Expressions and body language of those in photographs	Camera shots and focus; background

Adapted from Anstey and Bull 2006

Figure 2.17 Holly's text selections for her code-breaker lessons

Text Type	Semiotic System	Genre	Learning Purpose	What Students Need to Know	What Students Need to Be Able to Do
Roaring 20s Jackdaws Still images	Linguistic (captions) Visual Gestural Spatial	Photograph	Understanding what it means to be a code breaker	• What code breaking looks like • How to deconstruct or decode a text type and produce a caption that complements an image • Key historic, social, and political events of the era	• Break a photograph down into its smallest pieces of meaning • Interpret a visual to create summary text and predict significance of the photo as a whole image
Novel	Linguistic	Fiction	Understanding what it means to be a code breaker	See above	Use relevant vocabulary to identify comparisons between film and novel as they relate to authorial intent and characterization
Film	Linguistic Visual Auditory Gestural Spatial	Film	Examining the ways in which other texts portray the same story	See above	Use relevant vocabulary to identify comparisons between film and novel as they relate to authorial intent and characterization

Adapted from Anstey and Bull 2006

Figure 2.18 Holly's text analysis for her code-breaker lessons

*   *   *

With Holly, we visited a class of ninth graders who used both print and film clips from *The Great Gatsby*, examined photographs of the Roaring 20s, and discussed the central theme of the American Dream to become code breakers. Holly built upon methods teachers may be familiar with, such as anticipation guides and questioning – plus she used strategies for vocabulary, organization, and characterization – to help her students comprehend a particular theme and historic era.

Richard: Vietnam War Unit

In my media literacy course, my MTS unit centers on the American role in the war in Vietnam. This unit came about after I asked my students to examine two related media texts ("One Awful Night in Thanh Phong" and "Memories of a Massacre"). I use these texts because they give students a rich opportunity to put into practice many of the principles of media literacy. Earlier in the course, we had studied the key concepts of media literacy, which are:

- All media messages are constructions.

- The media construct versions of reality.

- Audiences negotiate meaning in media messages.

- Media messages contain commercial implications.

- Media messages contain ideological and value messages.

- Media messages contain social and political implications.

- Form and content are closely related in media messages.

- Each medium has a unique aesthetic form.

In addition, I taught students some of the jargon of deconstruction and media literacy: mass media, popular culture, status quo, media text, deconstruct, codes and conventions, genres, ideology, preferred reading, oppositional reading, cultural homogenization, target audience.

Finally, I introduced "the media triangle," a graphic organizer (see figure 2.19) that serves as a powerful tool for getting into shape as code breakers for all manner of mediated texts. It clearly illustrates three concepts essential to decoding any effective text: (1) the producer(s), (2) the intended audience, and (3) the text itself. I presented this graphic along with the accompanying questions, and, with my students, we used it as our guide to deconstruct various texts.

By the time the students understood this language (we had practiced contextualizing these with various brief, stand-alone texts), they were ready to develop their skills through sustained practice with denser, more complex, inter-related texts.

Over time, this unit has grown from the two seminal texts previously noted to nearly a dozen texts in various media and genre, including short fiction, a nonfiction feature article from *The New York Times Sunday Magazine*, videotape of a television news magazine show, period photographs, songs from popular culture, U.S. military "pocket rules," eye-witness historical accounts from Congressional investigations, an excerpt from a high-school psychology textbook, and a multi-panel "cartoon."

Text Questions

1. In what ways does this text tell a story? Does it connect to a larger story?

2. What type or category of story is it? Does it follow a formula?

3. What codes and conventions are used?

4. What are the characters like? Are they realistic? Are they stereotypes?

5. How do the characters relate to each other in terms of power, age, gender, race, and class?

6. What are the values and ideology of the characters? To what extent do I share these beliefs?

Production Questions

1. Where does this text come from? Who created it? Who owns it?

2. How is this text distributed or sold to the public? Who profits?

3. How was the text made? What production techniques were used?

4. What rules and laws affect this text? Is there an expected running time for a film or song? Are there any copyright marks or trademarks used to protect certain words or products?

5. How could I produce a similar text?

The Media Triangle

Text

Production

Audience

Audience Questions

1. How does this text appeal to me? What things do I like? What do I dislike?

2. Who is the intended target audience?

3. How and why does this text appeal to its audience?

4. In what different ways do people use or consume this text?

5. How could I change the text to make it more enjoyable?

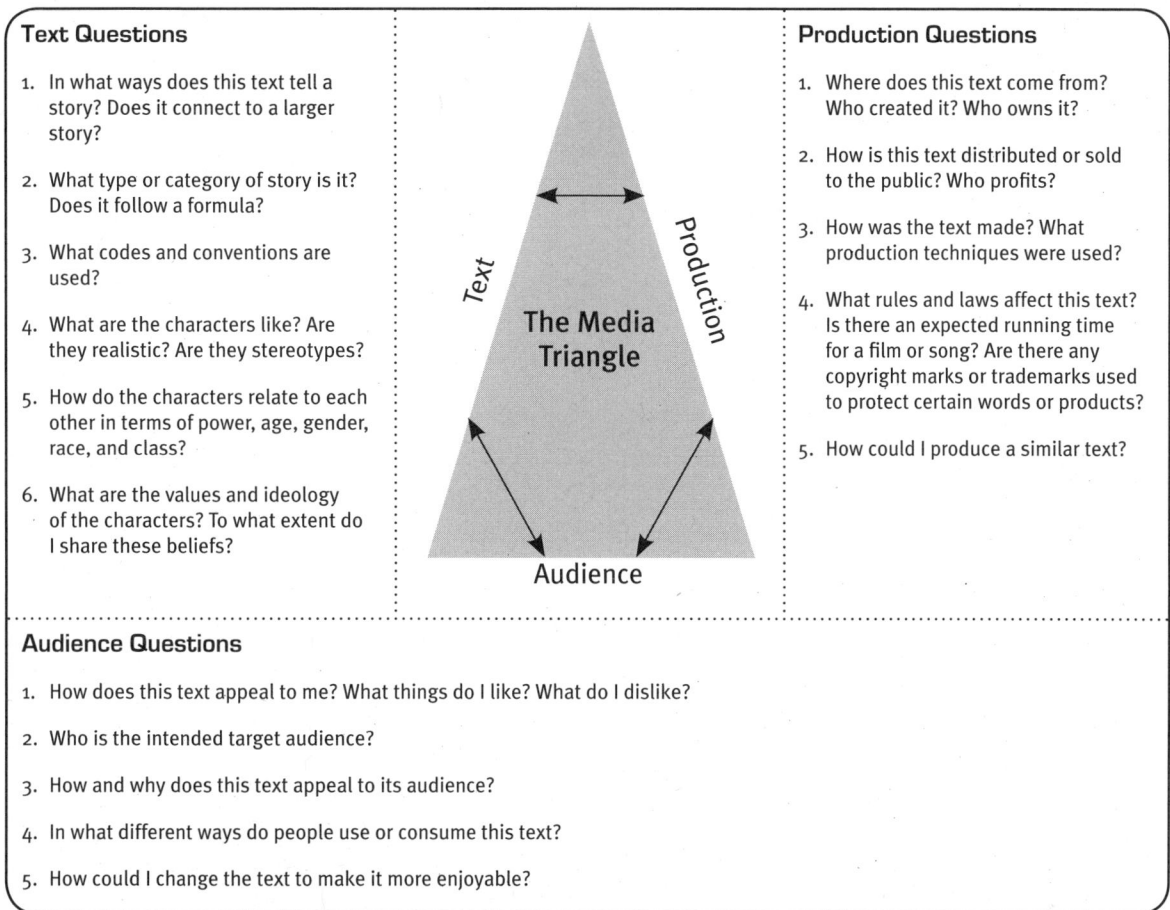

Figure 2.19 This graphic organizer is a powerful tool for decoding any effective text.

My purpose with this unit is to help my students negotiate a complex series of engaging – and conflicting – texts that center on events that occurred during the war in Vietnam. I suppose my most fundamental intent is to help my students arrive at a kind of "inner truth" – derived from careful literal and inferential meaning-making through a variety of texts, and its implications for negotiating meaning from their contemporary mediated world. I present them with a set of essential questions that serve as the boundaries of the field on which I ask them to practice their code-breaking, meaning-making, text-using, and text-critiquing skills. These questions are:

1. How do media affect our interpretation of a news story?
2. How do multiple perspectives (for example, different media) shape our perception of the truth?
3. What constitutes a war crime?

The first work I ask my students to do is to "warm-up" or activate their prior knowledge of Vietnam. Most have some fragmentary knowledge and awareness of the war in Vietnam; some have expansive and substantive knowledge. The graphic organizer (see figure 2.20) helps them collect what they do know.

In this space, write down any knowledge you may have about Vietnam by topic.	In this space, write down what you may need/want to know in order to understand the war in Vietnam.	In this space, write down anything new that you have learned. Include specific dates, references, and vocabulary.
Dates (start? major escalations? end?):		
Geography/culture:		
Reasons for the war:		
Who were the combatants? Who fought the war for the U.S.? Who fought the war for Vietnam?		
Who was in charge (for Vietnam? for the U.S.?)		
How was the war fought (By whom? With what means/weapons?)		

Side A – please turn over!

In this space, write down any knowledge you may have about Vietnam by topic.	In this space, write down what you may need/want to know in order to understand the war in Vietnam.	In this space, write down anything new that you have learned. Include specific dates, references, and vocabulary.
How many soldiers were killed/wounded?		
What was going on "back in the States" (in popular culture, politics)?		
How was the war reported?		
Who won this war?		
What were/are some of the songs, books, films that tell the story of Vietnam?		
What are some of the results or consequences of this war for you as a young American citizen?		

Side B

Figure 2.20 In this graphic organizer, students activate their prior knowledge about the Vietnam War.

From this chart, we collect the vocabulary of our shared experiences and create a word wall in our classroom. The terms are defined and illustrated as clearly as we are able with our beginning knowledge. Students are often eager to share what they do know from their reading, film viewing, study of history, popular culture, and family stories. I include words and phrases I know will present themselves in the MTS of the unit. In addition, I share with students a simple map of Southeast Asia and a timeline of the United States' association with Vietnam, beginning in the 1950s.

Once we have a baseline awareness of Vietnam, I ask students to respond quickly – not deliberately – to the statements in the anticipation guide (see figure 2.21).

Anticipating a Variety of Texts About Vietnam

Directions: *Before* reading the text, read following statements. Quickly indicate with an "A" those statements with which you agree; indicate with a "D" those with which you disagree. Be prepared to support your opinions with examples (from your own reading, work, or life experiences). *After* reading the text, check the column labeled "Author" for those statements with which you feel he or she would agree.

	You	Author
1. It is acceptable to kill innocent people (even women and children) during wartime.	____	____
2. The rules of war are clear and specific.	____	____
3. Memory is "always a liar."	____	____
4. Words are more important than deeds.	____	____
5. Eyewitnesses offer the most accurate testimony.	____	____
6. Accepting responsibility for one's actions is a means to forgiveness and reconciliation.	____	____
7. Justice delayed is justice denied.	____	____
8. Post-traumatic stress disorder victims cannot provide reliable testimony.	____	____
9. Special forces of the military (e.g., Green Berets, Navy Seals) are expected to engage the enemy in whatever way is necessary.	____	____
10. The media's role in war is to provide an unbiased point of view.	____	____

Figure 2.21 Anticipation guide

I solicit students' responses to each of the statements in the anticipation guide; most are willing to weigh in at this point – their curiosity is piqued – and we revel in the distinctive responses without evaluation or censure.

I provide students with a brief summary of some of the tragic stories in the historical accounts of Vietnam, including what happened with 25-year-old Lt. Bob Kerrey's commando team in Thanh Phong in 1969.[3] The first text we examine is a multi-panel, black-and-white political cartoon, "Bob [Kerrey] Goes to Thanh Phong" by author/artist Joe Sacco (see figure 2.22).

The cartoon is a visual format familiar to many high-school students. I project a screen-size digitized image of the text on the classroom wall and provide each student with his or her own desk copy. Because we have had some prior experience deconstructing visual texts in this course, students quickly employ these same practice strategies with this new text. To guide their practice, they work individually through a three-tiered graphic organizer (see figure 2.23) designed to support a deconstruction of visual texts.

Figure 2.22 Political cartoon by Joe Sacco

Courtesy of Joe Sacco

---

3. Bob Kerrey is a former governor of Nebraska, former U.S. senator, and was a candidate for the Democratic presidential nomination in 1992.

LEVEL 1

Visuals	Words
1. List the objects or people you see in the cartoon.	1. Identify the cartoon caption, author, and title.
	2. Locate three words or phrases used by the cartoonist to identify objects or people within the cartoon.
	3. Record any important dates or numbers that appear in the cartoon.

LEVEL 2

Visuals	Words
2. Which of the objects in your list above are *symbols or codes or conventions*?	4. Which words or phrases in the cartoon appear to be most significant? Why do you think so?
3. What do you think each *symbol* or *code* means?	5. List adjectives that describe the emotions portrayed in the cartoon (think **tone** here).

LEVEL 3

Describe the action taking place in the cartoon.

Explain how the words in the cartoon clarify the *symbols or codes.*

Explain the message of the cartoon.

What special interest groups would agree with the cartoon's message *(preferred reading)*? Why?

What special interest groups would disagree with the cartoon's message *(oppositional reading)*? Why?

Adapted from the U.S. National Archives & Resources Administration http://www.archives.gov/digital_classroom/lessons/analysis_worksheets/cartoon.html

Figure 2.23 Worksheet for deconstructing and analyzing a cartoon. This tool helps students use the structural conventions and patterns in the cartoon to decode how the words and images in combination create meaning and tone.

Richard's Code-Breaker Lessons

Instructional Disposition	Code Breaker	Teaching Examples	Examples of Students' Work
Writing Practices	Uses text conventions to write and communicate in different genres and text forms for different purposes	I model background knowledge derived from multiple sources and media.	Students develop short-answer responses to questions and statements regarding their prior knowledge of the U.S. role in Vietnam.
Discussion Across Texts	Participates in social and academic talk to communicate and express thinking about different text forms, patterns, and conventions	I model possible responses to anticipation guide.	Students share their own responses.
Vocabulary	Recognizes and uses vocabulary within contexts, content areas, or situations	Class-generated word wall of Vietnam War-specific vocabulary and jargon	Students research definitions.
Intertextual Connections	Recognizes and synthesizes patterns and conventions across texts and the different meanings within different forms and contexts	I present strategies of breaking codes and conventions of a graphic text supported by print text.	Students practice breaking the code of the cartoon by recognizing the patterns and various codes and conventions used by the author.
Engagement	Actively participates in decoding and encoding both familiar and new text forms	I provide worksheet for deconstructing a visual for students.	Students initiate their code-breaking individually, then pair-share their responses to the worksheet with another student.
Reading Practices	Develops identities that incorporate routines that value competence in breaking the code across all texts types	I model inference-making and code-breaking strategies based on vagaries of the cartoon.	Students compare responses to the cartoon and develop new inferences and understandings of the text.

Figure 2.24 This chart shows how Richard integrated all of the instructional dispositions into his code-breaker lessons.

Lesson Aims	Lesson Sequence Details
I want my students to: • Activate prior knowledge and lessons • Understand the role of the reader as a code breaker, using the metaphor of an athlete • Anticipate the challenges of deconstructing a text • Engage their own knowledge, skill sets, and patterns of practice as readers of text • Recognize familiar and obvious patterns, codes, meanings • Identify or synthesize new or different ideas, patterns, or meanings in the text	1. Remind students of the essential questions of the unit, the prior knowledge of the Vietnam War they charted in their graphic organizer, and the collection of Vietnam-era vocabulary on our word wall. 2. Present the "athlete" metaphor. Remind students that they have their own practices and patterns of play when it comes to successfully competing in any game. Distribute the anticipation guide for Vietnam texts. To extend the metaphor, suggest that the 10 statements are similar to the "pre-game" practices and habits most athletes cultivate. 3. Ask students to read each statement and respond quickly with little deliberation, working intuitively and emotively. Clarify any language or vocabulary questions based on the statements. When all have finished, solicit responses to each. 4. Display multi-panel cartoon, "Bob Goes to Thanh Phong." Read aloud the text to students, then distributes the three-tiered graphic organizer. 5. Ask students to work independently to complete the graphic organizer as they re-read and study the text. Urge them to respond as completely and as specifically as they can. All of the visual information means something! 6. Ask students to compare their responses with two other students. They should note shared or common responses, but especially pay attention to any data or information that are not common or questions or statements that elicit confusion, misunderstanding, or unique interpretations. Make note of all such distinctions. 7. After allowing time for this small-group discussion, again draw the whole group's attention to the text. Solicit responses to each of the statements or questions in the graphic organizer. Students may quickly note which parts of the deconstructed text reveal shared patterns of response or conventions. Where there are disagreements, allow opportunity for students to note them, and to reveal how they broke the code of the author's text, and how they interacted differently with the text or synthesized its meaning in other ways. 8. Return to the anticipation guide. Ask students to complete the column labeled "author" and to be prepared to defend their answers to the class based on the deconstructed text.

Figure 2.25 Richard's code-breaker lesson plans – at a glance

Text Type	Linguistic (oral/written language)	Visual (still/moving images)	Auditory (music/sound)	Gestural (facial expression/body language)	Spatial (layout/organization of objects in space)
Drawings from multi-panel political cartoon, "Bob Goes to Thanh Phong," by Joe Sacco	Each of the seven separate panels contains words in various syntactic patterns; some contain Arabic numerals	Black-and-white line drawings; students need to focus on all drawn information: foreground, middle ground, background	N/A	Some of the people in the drawings can be analyzed in terms of gesture, body language, and facial expression.	The arrangement of the subjects and other objects within the drawings
English language text that provides the spoken narrative and dialogue of the cartoon	Written text that provides provocative rhetorical questions, Vietnam War jargon, and affective meanings	Text size varies a bit (suggests emphasis).	N/A	N/A	Text is arranged in each panel in a conversational chronological order

Adapted from Anstey and Bull 2006

Figure 2.26 Richard's text selections for his code-breaker lessons

Text Type	Semiotic System	Genre	Learning Purpose	What Students Need to Know	What Students Need to Be Able to Do
Drawings from multi-panel political cartoon, "Bob Goes to Thanh Phong," by Joe Sacco	Linguistic Visual Gestural Spatial	Visual Nonfiction	• Engage students' own knowledge, skill sets, and patterns of practice as readers of text • Recognize familiar and obvious patterns, codes, meanings • Identify or synthesize new or different ideas, patterns, or meanings in the text	• Specific vocabulary • What code breaking looks like • How to deconstruct the patterns of imagery and language • How to use own personal experiences and background knowledge to interpret and synthesize new meanings from texts	• Read the language and drawings and derive meaning from them • Understand that each individual reader may perceive the meaning differently • Be able to articulate their own "broken code" of the text
English language text that provides the spoken narrative and dialogue of the cartoon	Linguistic Visual	Personal Nonfiction			

Adapted from Anstey and Bull 2006

Figure 2.27 Richard's text analysis for his code-breaker lessons

* * *

Richard used MTS to focus on Vietnam with junior and senior high-school students. In his code-breaking sessions, he juxtaposed a number of different texts on the same topic to provide students with a wide range of perspectives on one event. He coached the students through the process of negotiating meaning and placed special emphasis on learning and using vocabulary of the discipline and the Vietnam unit. Like athletes, they integrated a number of different skills: vocabulary, prior knowledge connections, using visual cues (comic) to code, and discussion to break the code. The students used code breaking to analyze and discuss each perspective.

PLANNING FOR THE CODE-BREAKER ROLE

In this chapter, you have read lessons from teachers of three different grade levels: Stephanie's code-breaker lesson on Americana with middle-school students, Holly's lesson on the Great Gatsby and the American Dream with ninth graders, and junior and senior students in Richard's unit on Vietnam. Each focused on teaching students how to code break challenging texts.

The questions we asked you to consider at the beginning of this chapter are listed again. Examine and apply the questions to your own planning of a code-breaking lesson within MTS.

1. How are my students thinking like athletes and code breaking the text?
2. How do I plan to support and encourage students to maintain and effectively use this role in their learning and monitoring?
3. Where will I integrate this role in my own practice?

Create your own lesson-plan and text-selection charts (see BLM 2 and BLM 3, appendix B). After you have drafted your code-breaking lessons, use the analysis chart (see BLM 4, appendix B) to analyze the lessons.

Chapter

Archaeologist as Meaning Maker

3

Meaning-making practices are used to make literal and inferential meanings of texts...a student must draw on and use meaning-making resources and code-breaking resources. The student's literacy identity – all previous literacy, social, cultural, and technological experiences – is the major resource for meaning making. The context in which the literacy activity takes place also influences meaning making... Meaning making is not simply about having or not having the resources; it is about knowing how to adapt or recombine them or use a strategy to work out how to use the resources already acquired (Anstey and Bull 2006, 45).

Luke (2000) and Anstey and Bull (2006) explain meaning making as thinking processes that are framed by each reader's cultural and social beliefs and experiences – including community, school, and popular culture. As students participate in the role of meaning maker, they work toward understanding and composing meaningful written, visual, and spoken texts; they explore each text's interior meaning in relation to their own resources. When roles are taught and practiced in the context of MTS, students use meaning-making resources to compare, and they learn to recognize variations in language, structure, and content. In MTS, each text form is used as a scaffold to inform students' meaning making in subsequent texts.

When we introduce students to the role of meaning maker, we use the metaphor of *archaeologist* as meaning maker. An archaeologist's job is to bridge the visible (written records, artifacts, and remains) with the invisible (human ways of survival, religious beliefs, family structure, and social organization). Archaeologists articulate and explain those connections and understandings of human behavior across centuries to others – to make meaning of the past and the present. This analogy helps students think about the knowledge, cultural discourses, texts, and different meaning systems in the role of meaning maker. Both roles – meaning maker and archaeologist – involve gathering evidence from multiple sources to make meaning in *relationship* to all of the evidence.

Archaeologists gather evidence and study internal structures, content, and contexts to help them make meaning of the past. They use their own resources, the evidence, and the social and cultural practices present in the context of the way of life they try to study from the past.

For students to be effective meaning makers, they need to develop and practice the thinking processes and identity of a meaning maker. Teachers can plan for instruction that teaches students to understand and compose multiple text forms by helping them use and acquire the knowledge to construct meaning from different texts (similar to studying a way of life) and relating it to their own knowledge and experiences of other text forms. To do this they need to gather text evidence (like an archaeologist collects evidence of the past), study it as a concrete, tangible text, and then consider it as a social and cultural artifact influenced by composition, design, and context.

In this chapter, we continue our classroom examples, with studies of meaning making within MTS. The meaning-maker portion of the chart in chapter 1 that compares the instructional dispositions and literacy practices is reprinted here to use as a frame to follow the examples (see figure 3.1 and figure 3.2).

Instructional Disposition	Meaning Maker
Writing Practices	Uses understandings to compose and design meaningful texts for various audiences and purposes
Discussion Across Texts	Participates in social and academic talk that deliberately integrates prior knowledge with new knowledge to make connections across text types and generate new, communal meanings
Vocabulary	Recognizes variations in language across contexts to understand and compose meaning in a wide range of genres and content areas
Intertextual Connections	Recognizes and compares the structures, responses, and possible readings across texts in different contexts
Engagement	Actively participates in reading and writing to make meaning and think about a range of meanings across text forms
Reading Practices	Develops identities that include the use of meaning-making tools and prior knowledge to understand content in different contexts

© 2010 Strop and Carlson

Figure 3.1 This chart shows the intersection of the instructional dispositions and the literacy practice of meaning maker.

Role (description)	Practice (questions)	Scaffold (literacy)	MTS (context)
Meaning maker (semantic competence): Takes part in understanding and composing all texts based on prior knowledge and experiences of other cultural discourses, texts, and meaning systems	• How do the ideas represented in the text string together? • What cultural resources can be used to make meaning? • What are the cultural meanings and possible readings?	Students are taught to bring their schemata and prior knowledge (based on culture, community, and gender) to texts; they also need to be taught to recognize and compare those to different genres, text structures, and schemata in new contexts.	

Adapted from Luke 2000; Luke and Freebody 1999; Anstey and Bull 2006

Figure 3.2 The literacy practice of meaning maker in multimedia text sets. The right-hand column can be filled in with examples from the topic being studied.

MEANING MAKER IN PRACTICE

As meaning makers, students learn to thinks like archaeologists who, after they gather the evidence, use meaning systems and their own experiences and prior knowledge to analyze it. The meaning maker accumulates evidence and the other cultural ways of knowing in order to understand and compose texts. The meaning maker then constructs meaning by reading and analyzing text using prior knowledge of text conventions, purpose, and context.

Below are lesson plans that illustrate the use and power of the meaning-maker format. First, Stephanie illustrates how meaning making is practiced with middle-school students during an Americana unit. Holly teaches ninth graders in an English class, and Richard's media literacy class crosses grade levels and ability levels in his high school.

While reading and analyzing each lesson, ask yourself the following questions:

1. How are my students thinking like archaeologists as they make meaning of the text?
2. How do I support and encourage students to maintain and effectively use this role in their learning and monitoring?
3. Where will I integrate this role in my own practice?

Stephanie: Americana Unit

Books and literature have been a life-long passion of mine. The most exciting aspect of reading, for me, is to dig deep into the text to discover something new about the present, the past, and the future. Each book, each poem, each dramatic script I read gives me passage into worlds and times I would not otherwise travel to. I feel so lucky to have this chance to "travel": The ancient writers from Greece and Rome teach me to think about the moral codes humans live by; the medieval writers inspire me to think about love, loyalty, and faith; and the writers from the age of enlightenment reveal the importance of knowledge, the dangers of knowing too much, and the necessity of experimentation. Each text we read connects us to a particular person or people, and time, but, because humanity links us all, these texts can still inform us about and have relevance to the lives we lead today.

For one of my meaning-maker lessons, I use the book that inspired my Americana unit: *Americana* by Hampton Sides. Sides is a journalist whose book surveys the United States, detailing the people, places, and events that he believes define the country. In his introduction, he describes America as "a crazy quilt of competing themes" and a "fecund mishmash of people" (2004, xii) – images that have really caught my imagination. Sides also talks about America's youthfulness, swagger, and a confidence that borders on arrogance. In just a few paragraphs, he provides the reader with multiple lenses through which America can be viewed. I like to find out what my students think of what Sides has to say, and I look forward to hearing their viewpoints and perspectives.

The lesson starts with a quick look back at the code-breaker lesson (see chapter 2). I ask students to choose the text types that are the most relevant to Hampton Sides' introduction. The students who worked on code breaking the novel, the poem, and the picture book are recalled and asked to present their ideas again on how to crack the code of their text type. Each of the three groups emphasizes the importance of breaking down the whole text into smaller pieces: words, phrases, or lines. The groups advise the students to look for the things that stand out or remind them of something they know about or have previously heard or seen. The students who had cracked the code of the poetry instruct the class to read and read again until the text makes sense. This is great advice (Sides' text is written for an audience beyond eighth grade, and it certainly posed a challenge for my eighth-grade readers). With this knowledge about how to read the nonfiction text in the forefront of their minds, students are ready to read and make meaning.

I ask students to read the text carefully and to highlight or underline anything that they find new, interesting, thought-provoking, or important. I also ask them to write a note next to their underlining or highlighting so that their ideas and reactions do not get lost or forgotten. Before they begin their reading, I model their task by highlighting, on the SMART Board, the line that stands out the most to me: Sides' (Ibid.) description of America as a "crazy quilt of competing themes." I explain that I like to quilt in my spare time. I also tell students that a crazy quilt is a unique kind of quilt, because the fabric, pattern, color, and shape of each piece can be different. Traditional quilting requires geometric lines and precise cutting and stitching; crazy quilting is the opposite. The United States is like a crazy quilt: it is a country of immigrants from all over the world whose different philosophies, beliefs, cultural practices, and cuisines exist together and compete with each other. I reference classical literature, Harlem poetry, reality TV shows, and the Food Network in my efforts to provide my ideas with specific reference points and examples. I tell students that a person does not have to conform to a particular size or shape or pattern in the United States; each has the freedom to be individual and different.

After I finish my example, I ask students if there is anything that stands out to them immediately upon looking at the text. I want to hand the power of meaning making over to the students, and my intent is that the students I ask will provide the other students with a bridge from dependence on the teacher to independent work. Inevitably, perhaps, the first student I called on chooses to focus on the following sentence (Ibid., xiii): "…waging war on sovereign nations in defiance of world opinion." This statement ignites a passionate debate as students in turn defend or argue against the American presence in Iraq. The meaning making has officially started. The students explore the text artifact (in this case, Hampton Sides' introduction) and link it to the "invisible realm" of human beliefs and social practices. To connect the text to their own lives, they use their own information resources – items they have seen on the news or read about on the Internet, the physical absence of a loved one on a tour of duty in Iraq or some other country, the content of political advertising campaigns. Students dig deep – not only into Sides' text – but into their own lives. It is exciting to watch. The text is no longer an alien mass of words; it is meaningful, contextual, and relevant to them.

When the class debate eventually subsides, I give the students 15 minutes to peruse the extract in its entirety, focusing on the details they find to be noteworthy. I had provided the students with the definitions of four words, and they are free to use the classroom dictionaries for any other words they are struggling with. Highlighters are also provided, and relevant doodling is permitted if a visual or image in their minds is strong. They are now ready for the class challenge.

The SMART Board has the extract displayed on its screen, and the highlighter utensil is ready for use. In turn, each student comes to the board, highlights a phrase that stands out for him or her, and gives a short, concise verbal presentation that explains why he or she has chosen that particular phrase. The students are also expected to provide examples that support their views. The catch? Each student has to present a unique word, phrase, or line unless he or she had something different to say about text that has already been highlighted. Class points are awarded for successfully completing the challenge, and students are permitted to respond to and (respectfully) debate the ideas presented. This task is designed with one key purpose in mind: to have students listen to multiple viewpoints, ideas, and perspectives, because there is rarely (if ever) one definitive answer or response to a text. Finding the intended meaning in reading, as in archaeology, would be an easy task if there was only one answer, one solution, to any kind of problem or question. In reality, meaning making is about putting the pieces together and creating a response from the evidence, just as an archeologist works to assemble the remnants of an artifact and tries to surmise its use and purpose and origin.

Following the presentations, students write their own one- to two-page definition of America. I ask them to think about Hampton Sides' introduction, the presentations they have listened to, and all the references and examples that have been named. I explain that they are to produce something that is meaningful and honest – not merely a piece of writing cranked out in a few moments. I give them an extra lesson to explore their ideas and write out their own definitions of America. At the same time that the students are writing their definitions, I write my own definition on the SMART Board. In this way, students witness meaning making in action.

Student examples:

Quote from Sides (Ibid., xii): "The older I get, the surer I am that I have no idea what American means."

Alicia: I don't agree with this phrase, because the older I get the more I learn and understand what America means. America means beauty. America means hard work from sun up to sun down. America means expressing your own individual feelings freely. America is one of the few countries that you could safely do that.

Quote from Sides (Ibid.): "Defining us is pretty much pointless."

Hilary: I think this is very true. There's so much about the U.S. that springs to one person's mind when they hear "America" might be unfathomably different from someone else's picture. We have nowhere near as long a history as a country like France or England, and yet, our story is like a woven tapestry from the three fates: brimming for colorful lives, stories, and seeming to stretch on indefinitely. Some things are indefinable and that's OK.

J.J.: America is a land of drastic contrasts. There are rich and poor, jolly and depressed, football stars and nerds, celebrities and convicts. With so many different people, cultures, and the like, it is impossible to accurately define America. For every viewpoint there is a different America. I'm just a kid... I try to view America as a whole, but even though that in itself is impossible, I also know that it is pointless to narrow it down. By focusing on just one point of view you run the risk of destroying all the others.

As students do this task, they are reentering the archaeological process – but at a different point in time. Now, they are the ones creating the "artifacts," texts that define who they are against the backdrop of their cultural past and present. It will be the task and responsibility of others in the future to read the meanings and find relevance to them. We make meaning when we read, but we also make meaning when we write.

The lesson plan (see figure 3.4) illustrates how easily the meaning maker builds upon the code-breaker lessons.

Stephanie's Meaning-Maker Lessons

Instructional Disposition	Meaning Maker	Teaching Examples	Examples of Students' Work
Writing Practices	Uses understandings to compose and design meaningful texts for various audiences and purposes	With students, I discuss Hampton Sides' definition of America and write my own definition of America to share with students.	Students produce their own written definition of America. They present their writing using a text type of their choice: poetry, prose, picture book, etc.
Discussion Across Texts	Participates in social and academic talk that deliberately integrates prior knowledge with new knowledge to make connections across text types and generate new, communal meanings	Students are given multiple opportunities to share their own point and to listen to the viewpoints of others. Debate is actively encouraged, and students are permitted to comment and discuss their peers' ideas.	• Individual presentations followed by student comments and questions • Sharing individual definitions of America and giving feedback to each other
Vocabulary	Recognizes variations in language across contexts to understand and compose meaning in a wide range of genres and content areas	I provide students with the definitions of complex words in Sides' introduction; for example: *fecund, protean, nuanced.*	• Code-breaker teams emphasize the importance of looking for words and phrases that trigger reaction. • Students look for words/phrases that trigger reaction in introduction. • Students have access to classroom dictionaries.
Intertextual Connections	Recognizes and compares the structures, responses, and possible readings across texts in different contexts	When I model response to Sides' introduction, I give specific intertextual reference points; for example: Food Network shows, MTV reality television shows, classical literature, and Harlem poetry.	• Students react to the introduction, noting down examples to support their ideas. • Students present their ideas to the class, giving examples from any text type to support their viewpoint.
Engagement	Actively participates in reading and writing to make meaning, and thinks about a range of meanings across text forms	I demonstrate and model my own enthusiasm and engagement by discussing my reaction to the introduction. I display relevance of texts to themselves.	• Each student participates in the class presentation challenge. • Each student actively engages in the writing process. • Each student shares his or her writing and receives feedback.
Reading Practices	Develops identities that include the use of meaning-making tools and prior knowledge to understand content in different contexts	I model how to arrive at an idea by making connections to personal experiences and a range of different texts.	When reading the introduction, students make connections between the text and their own lives, current/past events, and other texts.

Figure 3.3 This chart shows how all of the instructional dispositions are integrated into Stephanie's meaning-maker lessons.

Lesson Aims	Lesson Sequence Details
I want my students to: • Take on the role of meaning maker • Understand how to create meaning when reading texts • Understand how to make connections with the text • Practice creating their own meaning through writing	1. I introduce and explain the concept of the reader as meaning maker. 2. I explain that the lesson focuses on nonfiction written by a journalist called Hampton Sides. 3. I refer back to the code-breaking lessons. Which groups of code breakers should present their methods of code breaking to the class: The music video code breakers? The poetry code breakers? Students nominate and then vote for the most relevant groups to re-present their ideas. 4. Code-breaking groups present their ideas again. As a class, we discuss which ideas will help students read and understand the nonfiction extract the most. 5. Student task: Read the extract and highlight or underline anything that stands out as being new, interesting, though-provoking, or important information. Students are also to write a note explaining their ideas and give examples from real life or other texts to support their ideas. 6. Before students begin, I model by explaining one text moment that caught their attention. Reference personal life and a range of texts in modeled response. 7. Before students begin, I ask them if they have any immediate reactions to the text so that other students can aid the modeling of the task. I call on several students to explain their ideas. I then let students discuss and debate responses. 8. Students spend 15 minutes reading text, creating meaning, and making connections. 9. Class challenge: Each student has to present a different idea about the text to the rest of the class. Playing for class points. No repetition of ideas allowed. Once again, I permit students to respond to the ideas raised and suggested by each of the students. 10. Student task: I write my own definition of America. I also write my own definition alongside the students. If I make my writing public, I use the SMART Board, an overhead projector, or other device.

Figure 3.4 Stephanie's meaning-maker lesson plans – at a glance

Text Type	Linguistic (oral/written language)	Visual (still/moving images)	Auditory (music/sound)	Gestural (facial expression/body language)	Spatial (layout/organization of objects in space)
Extract from the introduction to *Americana* by Hampton Sides	Prose, word choice	Imagery used within the piece	N/A	N/A	N/A

Figure 3.5 Stephanie's text selections for her meaning-maker lessons

Text Type	Semiotic System	Genre	Learning Purpose	What Students Need to Know	What Students Need to Be Able to Do
Prose passage: Extract from the introduction to *Americana* by Hampton Sides	Linguistic Visual	Nonfiction	Understanding: How to create meaning when reading texts; how to create own meaning through writing	• How to code-break this text type: focus on specific words/phrases, re-read, highlight, annotate, look up words, etc • How to make connections between the text they are reading, their own lives, and the cultural texts that surround them • The role they play in making meaning – as readers, they are in a truly powerful position	• Read the text, and identify the words or phrases that strike them as being noteworthy • Articulate and express why a particular text moment stands out to them • Provide examples to support their ideas and comments • Express their own ideas, and create their own meaning via writing

Figure 3.6 Stephanie's text analysis for her meaning-maker lessons

* * *

The use of quotes is a powerful means of connecting readers to text, to everyday experiences, and, ultimately, to personal identity and awareness. Stephanie's students linked schemata and prior knowledge to texts based on American culture and community, and they began to recognize and compare different contexts within them. Stephanie posed questions about ideas, culture, and perspective. By quarrying more deeply into the meaning behind the words, her middle-school students developed voice, opinion, and point of view by actively participating in writing and articulating meaning.

Holly: Gatsby and the American Dream Unit

During the code-breaking practice, students developed ways of interpreting photographs of the Roaring 20s, acquainted themselves with the specialized vocabulary of the era, and examined F. Scott Fitzgerald's style, characterization techniques, and authorial intent. Students practiced "cracking the code" of both the written and film versions of *The Great Gatsby*. Like athletes, the students analyzed the playing field and scouted the competition. Now, as meaning makers, they will gather more evidence to understand Fitzgerald's purpose and themes. At the same time, they will continue to "unearth" the characters who inhabit the pages and scenes of the novel and film.

The Great Gatsby is considered testament to Fitzgerald's "discovery of and immersion in the psychic forces that drove life" (Thompson 1996) in the Jazz Age. Students connect most readily to this book as a cultural artifact when they start to compare their own dreams to those of Gatsby, Nick, Tom, Daisy, and other characters in the novel. To begin this lesson, I have students write a personal reflection on a goal or dream that has come to fruition. I ask them to describe how achieving that goal or dream may have seemed less satisfying than it had promised to be. The following prompts help structure their responses:

1. Describe what went into preparing for the dream or goal.
2. Was the dream tied to money, hope, and/or getting the person you wanted? If so, how?
3. Once the dream came to fruition, how long did the feelings of happiness last? What emotions followed the achievement of the dream or goal?

We then begin a study of chapters 4 through 9 of *The Great Gatsby* by building predictions and attempting to "assemble the main characters' profiles." This is similar to how an archaeologist examines artifacts in order to build hypotheses.

To start the process, I review how to identify a pivotal quote and analyze it for significance. I provide students with several important quotations spoken by or describing main characters, from both the novel and the film (Buehl 2001, 78).[1] I group students who are working on the same characters, and they attempt to identify trait descriptors to match the character quotes. They compare written notes with peers to create "body biographies." They also challenge themselves to find sophisticated adjectives and action verbs (what I call "expansion vocabulary") to represent these traits. For example, Gatsby is often cast as "tenacious," Daisy as "frivolous," and Tom Buchanan as "supercilious." This process of "predicting the profile and identity" of key characters continues as students complete the novel and finish viewing the film.

To increase the acuity of the lens they bring to the novel and the film, I assign each student one *Gatsby* main character to track (see figure 3.7). Just as an archaeologist in the field records descriptive notes, students examine the ethics, values, capacities for hope, and so on of their subjects, noting the context of those subjects' actions.

---

1. This is a strategy called "Character Quotes" from Buehl's (2001) strategy book.

Written Explanation of Wilson Body Biography

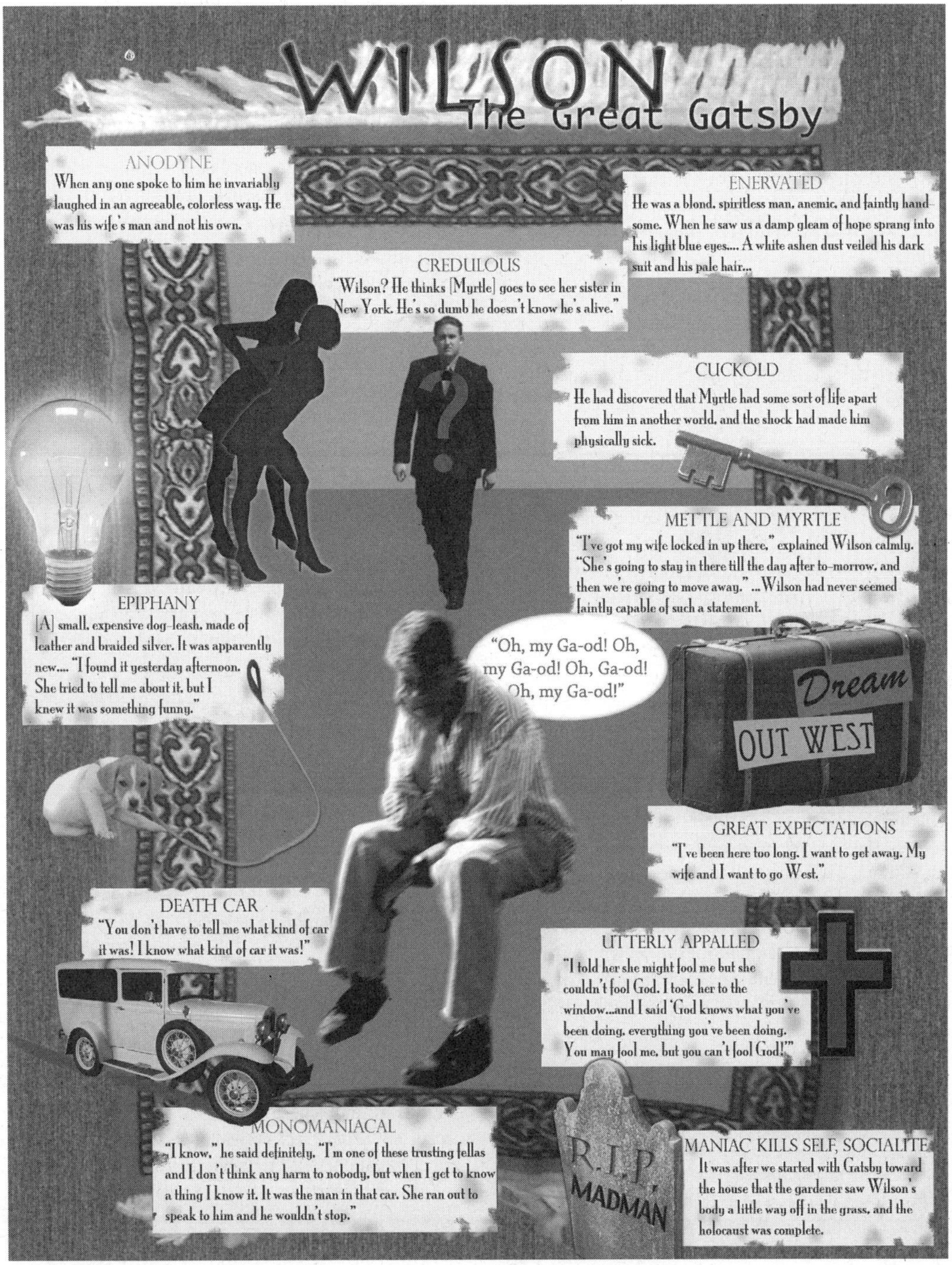

Courtesy of Layli Amerson

Figure 3.7 (and on following two pages) Layli, one of Holly's students, created this body biography.

Visual Elements

The visual elements in the body biography symbolize and represent aspects of the plot as related to Wilson and of Wilson's internal and external character. The collage should be viewed from top to bottom, as it is arranged chronologically. The list below explains the images:

- The **background** resembles dust. Wilson is described as being covered with dust; similarly, his personality is "dusty." Bland, meek, and oblivious, it takes two traumatic events (his realization of Myrtle's affair and her death) to blow that layer of dust off his inner being and drive him to action.

- The **carpet** in the background symbolizes Wilson's easily abused lack of suspicion. Myrtle and Tom walk all over him with their affair. Even after the affair ends, Tom dupes Wilson when he is seeking revenge by blaming Gatsby for Myrtle's death.

- The **colors** in the carpet (yellow to blue to red) symbolize a timeline of Wilson's emotional states. The **yellow** portion represents Wilson's initial enervated, threadbare status, as yellow traditionally represents decay and aging. The **blue** portion represents a time of major upheaval and distress in Wilson's life, after he discovers that Myrtle's leads two lives. He is so disconsolate at this realization that he becomes ill, hence the choice of blue to evoke sadness and depression. The **red** portion represents the final stage of Wilson's life, after Myrtle's sudden death. It represents his rage, vindictiveness, and overall visceral feelings. The pictures and text placed in the three areas correspond with the color they are nearest to, for the most part.

- The **flapper** represents Myrtle, who in many ways lives like a flapper, showing no regard for traditional social constraints. The flapper's exuberance represents Myrtle's vitality. Although Wilson and Myrtle don't have an honest marriage, it is Wilson's only relationship, and he loves his wife deeply. However, she leads a double life, as depicted by the two images of the flapper. She hides her life with Tom from Wilson, represented by the transparent flapper. His entire involvement in the events of the book revolves around her.

- The **light bulb** and **dog leash** represent Wilson's discovery of his wife's deception. The light bulb reflects Wilson's illumination. The fancy dog leash illustrates the cause of that illumination: Wilson finds the dog leash in a drawer and instinctively knows his wife is leading a life apart from him; why else would she need a leash? The discovery of the leash is a pivotal point in Wilson's life.

- The mysterious **man with the question mark** represents Myrtle's lover, whose identity remains unknown to Wilson after he discovers his wife's infidelity. Wilson tries to figure out who the culprit is in his blue period, questioning his neighbor Michaelis just before Myrtle's death.

- The **key** represents two aspects of Wilson. On the more literal side, it represents his choice to lock up Myrtle after he detects her dishonesty. Figuratively, it symbolizes the previously unexposed store of decisiveness and focus that the shock of his discovery unlocks. This released determination brings him out of his usual stupor.

- The **suitcase** symbolizes Wilson's new plan and dream: to move "out West." He hopes that getting away from the East will terminate his wife's relationship with her lover. Although the author doesn't delve much deeper into Wilson's reasons for planning to leave, it is clear that he wants to continue life with Myrtle, as he vows to bring her along. To speculate, moving out West is Wilson's newfound American Dream: to leave his old life behind, erase the problems of his marriage, and live not as a cuckold but as the master of his wife. "Out West" is a blank slate to him, a naïve and desperate hope.

- The shivering, **distressed man** in black and white represents Wilson after Myrtle's death. This image evokes Wilson's extreme anguish throughout the night of her death, a transformation from his hardened attitude before the accident.

- The **cross** symbolizes Wilson's invocation of God. He is not a religious man—he tells Michaelis that he hasn't been to church since his wedding. When he reprimands Myrtle for her deception and betrayal, he tells her that God sees everything even if she pulls the wool over Wilson's eyes. This demonstrates the extent of his shock at Myrtle's disloyalty, and also the depth of the injury that Myrtle has done to him. Perhaps most importantly, it reveals a side of Wilson that hadn't yet come out—moral rectitude rather than bland passivity.

- The **yellow car** represents the car that killed Myrtle (Gatsby's car). Wilson becomes fixated on this car after his initial lamentation. It is highlighted in red to represent Wilson's belief that the driver was intentionally malicious. The **drops of blood** falling from it signify the carnage that results from the hit-and-run. The car kills Myrtle, but this leads to the deaths of both Wilson and Gatsby, as, driven to desperation, Wilson wreaks his vengeance and snuffs out his own sorrow.

Figure 3.7 (cont'd)

- The **gravestone** represents Wilson's suicide. Crazed by Myrtle's death, speculating on connections between the driver and his late wife, he searches out the owner of "the death car," Gatsby, and murders him. Then he commits suicide. The inscription of "madman" on the gravestone represents the way the newspapers presented him: a psychotic man "deranged by grief." He dies as one-dimensional as he started.

Text Evidence

The text evidence serves to highlight the main points of the plot in which Wilson was involved, and to expose his character at multiple stages of development. After pulling out many quotes about Wilson from the original text, I narrowed my choices down to the most relevant and informative. There are more pieces of original text than are required, and many overlap required categories. Some don't provide insight into Wilson's character, but they do explain his involvement in the plot, and therefore create a cohesive, precise picture of Wilson overall. I tried to create the feeling that the viewer is reviewing bits and pieces torn from *The Great Gatsby*, attempting to understand Wilson like a detective. The pieces of text will be referred to by their headings on the body biography.

- "Mettle and Myrtle," "Utterly Appalled," and "Monomaniacal" contain the most introspective lines of **Wilson's dialogue**. They best illustrate the change in his character from mild to assertive, and his emotional responses to the trauma he undergoes. These changes allow his mettle to break the surface of his bland character. The other pieces of dialogue, "Great Expectations" and "Death Car," are also crucial. "Great Expectations" makes Wilson's American Dream (discussed above) explicit, and also extends the idea contained in "Mettle and Myrtle." "Death Car" alludes to a key turning point in the plot (Myrtle's death) and sets up Wilson's manhunt for his wife's killer. Finally, the text in the white circle ("Oh, my Ga-od!") is the most trenchant and raw of any of Wilson's lines. He repeats this mantra over and over compulsively, wailing with intense grief. There is no point in the book other than this when the reader sympathizes with Wilson more; his tortured cry proves his capacity for pain.

- The other pieces of **original text** convey views of Wilson's character by others, as well as significant points of the plot. "Anodyne," "Credulous," and "Enervated" reveal aspects of Wilson's character while he is still in the dark about Myrtle's affair, presenting background on his appearance, mannerisms, and ignorance. "Cuckold," "Epiphany," and "Maniac Kills Self, Socialite" present events that change the course of Wilson's life: his discovery of Myrtle's duplicity, and his murder/suicide. Both the excerpts of "Cuckold" and "Epiphany" warranted inclusion even though they were about the same event because "Cuckold" generalized the event, while "Epiphany" demonstrated Wilson's instinct, which is perhaps an unexpected trait in such a desiccated man.

Bibliography

Asquith, Malcolm. "Crossley Cars of the 1920s." 2004. 30 Mar. 2009.

Blanken, Lorain. "Religious and Expressive Stencils." *About. com: DIY Fashion*. 30 Mar. 2009.

"British Army Suitcase." *Field Textiles Company*. 30 Mar. 2009.

"Flapper Costume & Accessories." 30 Mar. 2009.

"Gravestone." *Image Chef*. 30 Mar. 2009.

"The Great Gatsby." *Sky Entertainment*. 30 Mar. 2009.

"Iraq Rug: 1930's Precedent for Map Rugs Showing Provinces." *Afghan War Rug Blog*. 22 June 2007. 30 Mar. 2009.

"Metal gold braided dog leash heavy fancy mesh." *EBay*. 30 Mar. 2009.

"Old Key." 9 July 2007. 30 Mar. 2009.

Pittman, Adrian. "A Great Idea." *Module*. 29 Dec. 2008. 30 Mar. 2009.

Figure 3.7 (cont'd)

I help students identify film scenes and novel passages that reflect evidence of how Fitzgerald's characters pursue the American Dream. As the character tracking is completed, students who are investigating the same characters are grouped to discuss ideas. Each then produces a body biography and presents it to the class (see BLM 5 and BLM 6, appendix B). This assessment is structured to also assist students in the American Dream panel interview (a summative assessment) (see chapter 4). It is important to note that, like archaeologists piecing together evidence, students reflect a continued search for verification of their hypotheses in their body biographies. Also, like archaeologists, the students alter information to match the most recent evidence.

Holly's Meaning-Maker Lessons

Instructional Disposition	Meaning Maker	Teaching Examples	Examples of Students' Work
Writing Practices	Uses understandings to compose and design meaningful texts for various audiences and purposes	I model choosing significant quotes and the criteria that make them so. I structure a "Character Quotes" exercise as a way of raising student interest in characters and as a way of structuring predictions.	• Students work with significant quotes that I provide, predicting in writing whose words are captured and what traits may be reflected in those words. • As reading progresses, student groups create "body biographies" and match Character Quotes respectively.
Discussion Across Texts	Participates in social and academic talk that deliberately integrates prior knowledge with new knowledge to make connections across text types and generate new, communal meanings	I model the steps of attaching quotes to characters as a "body biography" is built.	Students meet in groups to compare predictions tied to Character Quotes exercise. After generating "body biographies," they present "highlights" of their findings to whole class and note where and how their original predictions shifted.
Vocabulary	Recognizes variations in language across contexts to understand and compose meaning in a wide range of genres and content areas	I model labeling character traits with specific "expansion vocabulary" as the body biographies are built.	Students focus on comparisons between the book and film depictions of characters, focusing on expansion vocabulary describing key traits.
Intertextual Connections	Recognizes and compares the structures, responses, and possible readings across texts in different contexts	I choose scenes to "drill down into" as ones whose codes represent specific purposes that may exemplify character traits impacting the characters' pursuit of the American Dream (AD).	Students continue to apply knowledge of screen and print codes as they build comparisons between the film and novel, tracking character development and the pursuit of the AD.
Engagement	Actively participates in reading and writing to make meaning and thinks about a range of meanings across text forms	I ask students to make personal meaning in a reflection so they can think more deeply about the dreams of the characters in *The Great Gatsby*.	Students write to reflect on a personal goal or dream and how the dream tied to wealth, hope, and/or "getting the girl/guy/partner," etc.
Reading Practices	Develops identities that include the use of meaning-making tools and prior knowledge to understand content in different contexts	I ask students to adopt a particular purpose in reading so they can practice connecting their "film personas" with the development of their "book personas."	Students adopt the personas of main characters and closely follow those characters' developments by identifying pivotal quotes and by tracking ethics, values, capacity for hope, tactics to achieve dreams, etc. in both the film and the novel.

Figure 3.8 This chart shows how all of the instructional dispositions are integrated into Holly's meaning-maker lessons.

Lesson Aims	Lesson Sequence Details
I want my students to: • Take on the role of meaning maker • Understand how to create meaning when reading texts • Understand how to make connections with the text • Practice creating their own meaning through writing	1. Students generate a reflection on a dream or goal that has come to fruition but may not have held its promise. This prepares them to identify with the decay of Gatsby's dream. 2. To begin building profiles for the body biographies, I review identifying "pivotal" quotes and criteria for significance. Students complete Character Quotes exercise and compare findings with peers, analyzing the same *Gatsby* characters and the expansion vocabulary that describes those characters. Students work to become experts on multiple dimensions of their assigned characters. 3. Class discussion continues on the novel and the film to help students identify and discuss how Fitzgerald reflects his characters' pursuit of the American Dream. 4. Students complete body biographies.

Figure 3.9 Holly's meaning-maker lesson plans – at a glance

Text Type	Linguistic (oral/written language)	Visual (still/moving images)	Auditory (music/sound)	Gestural (facial expression/body language)	Spatial (layout/organization of objects in space)
Classic novel	Prose, dialogue, vocabulary, style	Book cover	N/A	N/A	N/A
Film	Dialogue, tone, volume, pitch, rate, regionalisms, slang of the era	DVD cover	Sound effects, music	Actors' expressions and movements	Actors' distance from each other ("social bubbles")

Adapted from Anstey and Bull 2006

Figure 3.10 Holly's text selections for her meaning-maker lessons

Text Type	Semiotic System	Genre	Learning Purpose	What Students Need to Know	What Students Need to Be Able to Do
Novel	Linguistic	Fiction	To establish concept of American Dream (AD) with classic literature and iconic characters	• How the Roaring 20s gave rise to a new AD • How the AD of the 1920s tied to wealth, hope, "getting the partner," etc.	• Use expansion vocabulary and prediction to describe characters based on what they say, do, and think • Generate character profiles and body biographies that portray how the main characters achieved or lost their dreams
Film	Linguistic Visual Auditory Gestural Spatial	Fiction	To examine the ways in which other texts portray the AD with the same iconic characters	How codes and conventions of film contribute to characterization and the interpretation of each main character's success with his or her personal dream	Articulate how the unique conventions of this film complement and contrast the characterization of the novel and the ways in which the AD is conceived and achieved or lost

Adapted from Anstey and Bull 2006

Figure 3.11 Holly's text analysis for her meaning-maker lessons

* * *

Similar to archaeologists, Holly's ninth graders worked to uncover and make meaning from the cultural artifacts presented to them. Holly used quotes from the text to extend students' thinking. She also guided her students through text, dialogue, film, and art to give them the tools to dig deeper into the meaning of the time period and the notion of the American Dream. In addition, by engaging her students in higher-level thinking, which advanced their comprehension of the social and cultural history of the era, students were able to undertake multilayered character analyses.

Richard: Vietnam War Unit

All of the texts in the Vietnam MTS help students acquire the knowledge they need to construct rich, contextualized meaning. However, a series of shorter, multimodal texts placed near the beginning of the unit helps students assemble these texts as artifacts – to examine them individually and to place them in relationships with one another to make fresh meaning(s). When presented with brief texts – fragments of "big picture truths" – practiced, in-shape students quickly put into play their code-breaking skills and make meaning from each single text, and then develop the synergistic meaning that the texts together can provide.

Examples of such texts that I share with my students include: *Village*, a short fiction by Estela Portillo about a young Hispanic soldier's reluctance to fire on a bucolic village in Vietnam; "The Massacre at My Lai," an American helicopter pilot's account of that actual event; a ground soldier's eyewitness account of the same wartime atrocity; a portfolio of selected iconic photographic images taken during the war; and various (pro-war and anti-war) songs that were part of the popular culture during the 1960s and 1970s.

In an effort to promote their meaning making, at the start of class, I charge the context of the classroom by playing Lt. Barry Sadler's "Ballad of the Green Beret" while projecting the lyrics on the screen. I inform students that this song was the number one hit in American popular music culture for five weeks in 1966, which was relatively early in the chronology of the Vietnam War. The song's patriotic lyrics and tone cast the U.S. military in a positive light. I do not routinely scaffold each similar text. Rather, I scatter them about our archaeological dig as fragments – shards – and let my students make meaning of them in the context of all the other artifacts.

I remind students of our three essential questions:

1. How do media affect our interpretation of a news story?
2. How do multiple perspectives (for example, different media) shape our perception of the truth?
3. What constitutes a war crime?

As in the first lesson, we collect and define unfamiliar vocabulary from each print text. Words such as *barrio, pyre, garrote, court-martial*, and *communiqué* are added to our word wall.

We then read the fiction, *Village*. In this story, a young soldier, Rico, sees far too much of his own barrio back home in the Vietnamese village that his unit is ordered to destroy. He refuses to open fire. Instead, he deliberately wounds his commanding officer. The attack is thwarted; Rico is imprisoned and scheduled for court-martial.

After reading the story, each student writes responses to a set of questions. Then, I place students together for a brief "pair-share" of their responses. Finally, I guide them through a whole-class discussion based on the following discussion questions:

1. What conflicts does Rico experience at the beginning of the story?
2. Why does Rico think that following orders would be "the easy thing to do"?
3. Do you think Rico did the right thing? Why? Why not?
4. How do you think Rico will explain his actions at his court-martial?

As you might imagine, there is little agreement, let alone consensus, on question three, but the conversation is invariably rich and weighted with students' own contexts – their values and ideologies. In their role as archaeologists, students are sometimes disturbed and always enthralled by what they have found. They are ready to look at some more "artifacts."

Next, we read back-to-back eyewitness accounts of the My Lai atrocity. At first, student reaction seems muted. The juxtaposition of these true stories with Portillo's fiction is sobering. Using similar questions (see above), we consider the two new texts. This time, students are much less ambiguous about doing "the right thing." There are far fewer rationalizations of the soldiers' actions.

Additionally, we look at a variety of wartime photographs. I project the photographs on a large screen, and students work at their desks with a three-step worksheet for each photo (see figure 3.12): observation, inference making, and questions. Just as on-site archaeologists divide a dig site into numbered grids to isolate soil sections and create more manageable focal points, students divide the photographs into quadrants to see what new details become available as they examine each more closely. They collect and record the specific data that they note: people, objects, activities, symbols/ codes/conventions. Then, based on their observations, they generate inferences. Finally, they respond to the following:

1. What questions does this photograph raise in your mind?
2. Where could you find the answers to your questions?
3. Who would publish or use this photograph and for what purpose?
4. How might different audiences use or react to the photograph?

Adapted from the U.S. National Archives & Records Administration <http://www.archives.gov/digital_classroom/lessons/analysis_worksheets/photo.html>. Photo: Courtesy National Archives, photo no. 111-SC-659354

Step 1: Observation

1. Study the photograph for two minutes. Form an overall impression of the photograph, and then examine the individual items in the photograph.
2. Divide the photo into quadrants, and study each section to see what new details become visible.
3. In the table below, list people, objects, activities, and symbols and codes (technical and symbolic) in the photograph.

People	Objects	Activities	Symbols and Codes

Step 2: Inference

Based on what you have observed above, list three things that you might infer from this photograph:

1.

2.

3.

Step 3: Questions

1. What questions does this photograph raise in your mind?

2. Where could you find answers to your questions?

3. Who would publish or use this photograph? For what purpose?

4. How might different audiences use or react to this photograph?

Figure 3.12 A worksheet for deconstructing and analyzing a photograph. When students observe images that are unfamiliar to them, they have many opportunities to speculate, raise their own questions, and begin to develop authentic and plausible meanings from the patterns that emerge from further discussion.

Richard's Meaning-Maker Lessons

Instructional Disposition	Meaning Maker	Teaching Examples	Examples of Students' Work
Writing Practices	Uses understandings to compose and design meaningful texts for various audiences and purposes	N/A	Students develop short answers to compelling questions that require careful analysis.
Discussion Across Texts	Participates in social and academic talk that deliberately integrates prior knowledge with new knowledge to make connections across text types and generate new, communal meanings	I model a thoughtful response to the questions posed after the short readings and after we analyze the photographs.	Students use their own short-answer responses to provoke further discussion by revealing their own meaning making, affirming meanings that their peers have already presented, or reacting to meanings with which they disagree.
Vocabulary	Recognizes variations in language across contexts to understand and compose meaning in a wide range of genres and content areas	I continue to collect useful vocabulary on our classroom word wall.	Students use this vocabulary as they create meaning from the various texts, often supplying specific information as they make inferences.
Intertextual Connections	Recognizes and compares the structures, responses, and possible readings across texts in different contexts	I present several texts in different media modes.	Students begin to move easily from print texts to visual texts to auditory texts to build layered inferences and make richer, more nuanced meanings.
Engagement	Actively participates in reading and writing to make meaning and think about a range of meanings across text forms	I often begin reading the Portillo story aloud, then hand it off to my students at their desks to complete.	Students, attracted by the opening song, and the first few paragraphs of the story, settle in to read and make meaning on their own.
Reading Practices	Develops identities that include the use of meaning making tools and prior knowledge to understand content in different contexts	I ask students to move from a fictional text to a set of nonfiction stories.	Students move seamlessly from fiction to eye-witness account, using the vocabulary and context clues they develop along the way.

Figure 3.13 This chart shows how all of the instructional dispositions are integrated into Richard's meaning-maker lessons.

Lesson Aims	Lesson Sequence Details
I want my students to: • Activate prior knowledge and lessons • Understand the role of the reader as a meaning maker, using the metaphor of an archaeologist • Develop a stance of curiosity regarding the artifacts and content of the lesson(s) • Engage their own knowledge, skill sets, and patterns of practice as readers of text • Recognize familiar and obvious patterns, codes, meanings • Make inferences from unfamiliar textual information • Raise questions and speculate about the purpose of the textual evidence • Identify or synthesize new or different ideas, patterns, or meanings in the text	1. I remind students of the prior knowledge of the Vietnam War and the vocabulary, texts, and essential questions of the unit. 2. I present the "archaeologist " metaphor. Note that an archaeologist gathers evidence from multiple sources to posit meaning(s) in relationship to the evidence. 3. I present the idea of the Green Beret – an elite, specially trained soldier in the U. S. Army, then play Lt. Barry Sadler's 1966 pop music hit, "The Ballad of the Green Beret." As students listen, I project the lyrics on the screen at the front of class. I ask no specific task of students (but I do respond to any questions they may have); it is what it is, an artifact of its day to be somehow placed into a broader context to discover its meaning. 4. I distribute print text "artifacts": the short fiction *Village* by Estela Portillo, and two eye-witness accounts of the massacre at My Lai. 5. I instruct students to read *Village,* collect unfamiliar vocabulary, and provide short-answer responses to a few questions. We review and discuss the vocabulary and the responses, particularly in regard to the actions of the story's protagonists, Rico. 6. I ask students to read both of the eye-witness accounts. I ask no specific task of students. I again respond to any questions they may have. These nonfiction texts are compelling – even challenging – in their graphic depictions and candor. I also point to the essential questions of our unit, which are written on the front board, and urge students to keep these in mind. Like archaeologists, they should speculate, pose questions, consider. These textual artifacts provide new evidence, other possibilities. 7. I distribute the worksheet for deconstructing and analyzing a photograph, and present a series of Vietnam-era wartime photos. A few are familiar – most students have seen them in their history books – but most are new images to them. I hold each image on the screen for a few minutes of close observation and ask student to record what they see in each image. Using their recorded data – the people, objects, activities, symbols, codes, and conventions – they then make inferences about each photo, and, finally, develop the kinds of questions an archaeologist might develop regarding this evidence. What questions do these photos raise in your mind? Where could you find answers to them? Who would publish or use this? For what purpose? How might different audiences (e.g., Vietnam veterans, Vietnamese people) use or react to these photos?

Figure 3.14 Richard's meaning-maker lesson plans – at a glance

Text Type	Linguistic (oral/written language)	Visual (still/moving images)	Auditory (music/sound)	Gestural (facial expression/body language)	Spatial (layout/organization of objects in space)
Song lyrics, "Ballad of the Green Beret" \ Prose short fiction, *Village,* by Estela Portillo \ Prose nonfiction: eyewitness testimonials of the My Lai massacre	All prose texts contain words in various syntactic patterns; some contain Arabic numerals	Song lyrics' image accompanied by an image of a U.S. Green Beret \ Fiction text accompanied by illustrative photograph of an unidentified Vietnam-era U.S. soldier	N/A	Stoic, iconic pride present in Green Beret image	N/A
Music, "Ballad of the Green Beret" \ Photographs: various images from the Vietnam War	Words of the song and language used \ N/A	Lyrics and soldier image presented \ Photos of Vietnamese villagers, landscapes, various soldiers, weapons of war, scenes showing the results of battle	Music and singer's voice; some sound effects \ N/A	Present in image of Green Beret \ Various expressions of body language and attitude of the people in the photos	N/A \ References to camera shots, points-of-view, focal points of imagery

Adapted from Anstey and Bull 2006

Figure 3.15 Richard's text selections for his meaning-maker lesson plans

Text Type	Semiotic System	Genre	Learning Purpose	What Students Need to Know	What Students Need to Be Able to Do
Lyric poetry (song lyrics)	Linguistic Visual Gestural Spatial	Poetry	• Engage their own knowledge, skill sets, and patterns of practice as readers of text \ • Recognize familiar and obvious patterns, codes, meanings \ • Identify or synthesize new or different ideas, patterns, or meanings in the text	• Specific vocabulary \ • What it means to be a meaning maker \ • How to examine disparate artifacts or evidence to form inferences, to speculate, to create meaning \ • How to use own personal experiences and background knowledge to interpret and synthesize new meanings from texts	• Read the language and drawings, and derive meaning from them \ • Understand that each individual reader may perceive the meaning differently \ • Be able to articulate their own meanings based on the collected artifacts or evidence of the texts
Various prose: short fiction, expository nonfiction	Linguistic Visual	Fiction			
Music	Visual Auditory	Personal nonfiction			
Still images	Visual Gestural Spatial	Photography			

Adapted from Anstey and Bull 2006

Figure 3.16 Richard's text analysis for his meaning-maker lessons

In his lessons, Richard guided his students through a variety of well-chosen texts, which contain "truths" about the Vietnam experience. He used higher-level questioning to focus students and empower them to speculate, contemplate, question, discuss, and make meaning of the pieces presented. The MTS he presented included a wide range of experiences – *New York Times* article, *60 Minutes* video, short fiction and nonfiction selections, music, photographs, and graphic organizers. Richard's use of these "artifacts" prompted his students to unearth new meanings and perspectives by gathering evidence from a mixture of different text styles.

PLANNING FOR THE MEANING-MAKER ROLE

In this chapter, you read Stephanie, Holly, and Richard's lessons that focus on challenging texts to engage students in meaning making.

The lessons demonstrate how to shift students more deeply into critical comprehension of texts. Students engage in reading, composing, and designing multifaceted texts. Like archaeologists, students construct meaning by uncovering hidden elements, asking and seeking answers to questions, and generating new meanings.

The examples in these lessons included whole-class discussion, group work, and independent writing during which meaning makers shared ideas, communicated new meanings, and designed meaningful texts to articulate thinking.

The questions we asked you to consider at the beginning of this chapter are listed again. Examine and apply the questions to your own planning of a meaning-maker lesson. After you have drafted your lesson, analyze it with the planning chart (see BLM 2, appendix B).

1. How are my students thinking like archaeologists as they make meaning of the text?
2. How do I support and encourage students to maintain and effectively use this role in their learning and monitoring?
3. Where will I integrate this role in my own practice?

Chapter 4
Tour Guide as Text User

Teaching pragmatic practices involves enabling students to read contexts of everyday use, assess how the technical features (e.g., genre, grammar, lexicon) of a text might be realized in these contexts, and size up the variables, power relations, and their options in that context (Luke 2000, 455).

Use texts functionally...by knowing about and acting on the different cultural and social functions that various texts perform inside and outside school, and understanding that these functions shape the way texts are structured, their tone, their degree of formality, and their sequence of components (Luke and Freebody 1999, 12).

Luke and Freebody (1999) explain that learning practices for the text user need to be held in context; texts are structured to be used for and function in different settings for different purposes for different people. For example, the content and construction of a text created for the purpose of entertaining children differs from a text that is created to teach medical students about diagnosis. A text for children's entertainment is created to appeal to children's aesthetic, imaginative responses to the sounds of language and the novelty of engaging, imaginary characters. A text for medical students' education in diagnosis is constructed to tap into their efferent (academic learning), knowledge base. Further, it builds on prior knowledge toward new understandings of diagnoses that are based on scientific knowledge and research. Each type of text is created for a different audience and is written in a unique way to serve its purpose.

When we introduce students to the role of text user, we use the metaphor of *tour guide* as text user. This metaphor helps the student think about the purposes, skills, and context necessary to this role. A tour guide plans a tour (context, audience) of, for example, a museum or a foreign country with a set of responsibilities. A tour guide needs deep knowledge of the context (museum or country) and of the group of people touring (school children or families on vacation, for example). Understanding the context includes knowing the people and the goals of the people being guided, and knowing the culture, language, geographical setting, history, and so on of the destination. Tour guides are paid for the knowledge they have of the context of the tour. A tour guide prepares for a tour by learning about the context and the details of navigating (code breaking) and appreciating (meaning making) the experience. The guide then combines that knowledge with the social and cultural settings of the tour and the social and cultural backgrounds and experiences of the tourists.

The text user recognizes the influence of text and understands the purposes and audiences for different forms of text. The text user understands that different texts are used for different purposes. For students to be effective text users, they need to develop and practice how texts are developed and consumed for different purposes. Text users think about how the text was constructed for particular purposes and are changed by the contexts within which they are presented and used. Text users need to recognize how the meanings of different texts are shaped by their form. For example, a warning about the dangers of cigarette smoking is shaped and formed differently on a pack of cigarettes, in an advertisement for the brand of cigarettes being sold, and in an article about lung cancer. Tour guides might find that some people in their group really enjoy a place but dislike the next stop in the tour. One group may respond very positively, be inspired by the touring, and interact with the people or knowledge encountered. Another group may find the same tour tedious or uninteresting to the point of being disengaged with the experience. Some tourists may build knowledge and understanding as the tour progresses, making each subsequent stop more interesting. Because of their enthusiasm, this same group may interact with others on the tour, so that they can share their experiences. Tourists in another group may be unable to bridge the gap between their own knowledge and the new context and become less and less engaged because they fail to gain any understandings as the tour progresses.

In this chapter, we present some classroom examples of practicing the role of text user by "touring" texts within MTS. The text user portions of figure 1.3 and figure 1.5, which compare instructional dispositions and literacy practices, are reprinted here for you to use as a frame as you follow the classroom lessons (see figure 4.1 and figure 4.2).

Instructional Disposition	Text User
Writing Practices	Uses knowledge to understand and shape writing by selecting different alternatives to fit social and academic situations
Discussion Across Texts	Participates in social and academic talk to differentiate and identify the purposes, uses, and contexts of different text forms
Vocabulary	Recognizes and uses vocabulary for different purposes and contexts
Intertextual Connections	Recognizes the construction and shapes of different meanings within and across text forms
Engagement	Actively participates in using background knowledge to inquire about and use different text forms
Reading Practices	Develops identities that use, analyze, and compare the way texts are shaped by intent and contexts

© 2010 Strop and Carlson

Figure 4.1 This chart shows the intersection of the instructional dispositions and the literacy practice of text user.

Role (description)	Practice (questions)	Scaffold (literacy)	MTS (context)
Text user (pragmatic competence): Knowing about and acting on the different cultural and social functions of various texts in and out of school (functions shape text structure, tone, purpose, organization)	How do the users of this text shape its composition? What do I do with this text, here and now? What will others do with it? What are my options and alternatives?	Students are taught to understand that texts are always situated in fields of economic, cultural, and social fields of power. Teach students to read contexts of everyday use – to assess how technical features are used in different contexts and power structures.	

Adapted by Luke 2000; Luke and Freebody 1999; Anstey and Bull 2006

Figure 4.2 The literacy practice of text user in multimedia text sets. The right-hand column can be filled in with examples from the topic being studied.

TEXT USER IN PRACTICE

As text users, students learn to think like a tour guide. Tour guides prepare for a tour by understanding the context of the tour, the people they guide, the purpose of the excursion, and how circumstances change as the tour moves from one place to another. Tour guides use their knowledge of the context and culture and of how tourists respond to different places and people. Tour guides understand that each encounter is different, because the people on each tour have unique responses.

The lesson plans that follow model how the role of text user is practiced in different grade levels with different types of texts in different contexts. Stephanie illustrates how text user is practiced with seventh graders in her Americana unit. Holly teaches *The Great Gatsby* and the American Dream with her high-school English students. Richard focuses on the war in Vietnam in a media literacy class that crosses grade levels and ability levels in his high school.

While reading and analyzing each lesson, think about or ask yourself the following three questions:

1. How are my students thinking like tour guides and using the text?
2. How do I support and encourage students to maintain and effectively use this role in their learning and monitoring?
3. Where will I integrate this role in my own practice?

Stephanie: Americana Unit

My Americana unit has taken a number of years to develop, and I still feel that it is not yet fully formed. The unit grows with the knowledge I acquire from paying attention to the news, the media, and the world around me. The unit is also influenced by my personal reading habits and the books and texts I read. I am always on the lookout for something new and different to use with my students. Imagine my excitement when I came across a great photography book called *Flag: An American Story*. The book is made up of photographs taken by photographer Lauri Lyons as she traveled America. She visited several states and, everywhere she went, she asked the people she met to pose with the American flag and write a short message about what they thought of America. Those photographed were free to choose their pose and free to write as they wished. I am so glad I found the book, and I am excited that I have had the opportunity to share the book with my students.

In preparation for the text-user lesson, I ordered several copies of the book – one for every three students. I then scanned a few of my favorite images into the SMART Board software so that I could share my thoughts and we, as a class, could discuss some of the photographs.

At the beginning of the class, I tell the students that the text type I am about to show them is image-based with a little bit of writing. I explain the layout of the book, and we talk about the role of the reader as a text user. I use the tour guide metaphor to explain the role of text user. I also use the metaphor to explain how we are going to tour the book *Flag*. First, I tell students that they will be touring every page of the book, spending time with each photograph, and visiting the writing that accompanies each picture. Second, I tell students they will tour the book as a whole, traversing the United States while seeing and meeting diverse groups of people across state, race, faith, and class lines. I explain that the America they witness in one photograph will not be the America they witness in the next photograph.

I then ask the students to nominate which code-breaker groups they want to present so that they have some tips on how to read image-based texts. The students recall the groups that presented on the photograph, painting, and graphic-novel text types. The picture-book group also contributes some information on how to read images. The advice given by the students in this group includes the following:

- Find the main subject.

- Explore the background.

- Look at the details beyond the main subject.

- Think about color and lighting, focusing on facial expression.

- Note the arrangement and placement of people in the photograph.

- Identify the kind of shot that has been used.

All of these things contribute to the message of the photograph. Another student adds that we need to pay close attention to the flag and how it is being held or presented by the people in the photographs. This is all great advice: before we begin the tours, we have acquired the knowledge and materials we need to get going.

Before I give students some independent reading time, we tour, as a class, the two levels mentioned above. I show the students one of my favorite photographs in the book. The photograph is of a man and four children. The home behind them does not look to be in the best shape. No one in the photograph is smiling, and one of the children looks ready to break away from the embrace of his father. Before I reveal the writing that accompanies the photo, I ask students to consider the following three questions as they tour this photograph:

1. What do you notice?
2. What information do you glean about the people in the photograph?
3. What do you think the author is trying to communicate through this picture?

The discussion is interesting, and students are concerned about the lack of happiness in the faces and the quality of the living conditions. Everyone notices the child who is pulling away from his father and thinks there might be some family issues here. One student points out that, sometimes, it is not what is in the picture but what is missing that is important. He assumes that the man in the picture is the children's father, and he wants to know where the mother is. When I reveal the note that accompanies the picture, the students learn the father had been absent for a period of time. We then spend time speculating where he has been and why he is back now. We all agree that this photograph shows just the beginning of a story, and we want to know more.

Like an archaeologist reconstructing a clay pot, we take on the role of meaning maker. We try to put together the family's story with just some of the pieces, but we find we need more to fully construct the story. The students think the author's message is that not everyone leads fully happy and fully complete lives. Some families have parents missing; other families deal with poverty and lack wealth. We need to be aware of what other people are going through instead of just focusing on ourselves.

The second photograph I show the students causes a debate. The photograph is of three boys standing against the backdrop of a ranch in Montana. The boys are smiling, and the landscape behind them is spectacular. Most students believe the author is sending a positive message about America and life in America. The United States has some of the most beautiful natural wonders in the world, and, while life can be busy and complicated, it can also be simplistic and idyllic. One student says that the place in the picture reminds her of her ideal home and lifestyle. (The next day she brought in a picture of a rundown ranch in Wyoming: she wanted to live there surrounded by countryside and animals. The photograph with the three boys had really struck a chord with her.)

However, not all of the students agree with her interpretation. Many say that the picture looks empty and isolated. They could not live there in that way, because they would feel cutoff from national and world events. These students feel that the author's message may be about the dangers of becoming too detached from the rest of society. It is interesting that the same stop on our tour has two very different effects on the audience.

We talk for a few minutes about our two photographic stops and the differences between them before I divide the class into groups of three to read the book. I ask each student to predict the following: (a) What other places and kinds of people do you think you will be visiting? (b) What do you think the author wants to show you? I want the students to see how each photograph has a meaning and a message. I also want students to see how each photograph contributes to the overall scheme of the book.

Each group of students has the rest of this first lesson to look at the remaining photographs in the book. The students record their thoughts of the photographs that really stand out and mean something to them. They can use the three questions from earlier in the lesson to help shape their thoughts and ideas: What do you notice? What information do you glean about the people in the photograph? What do you think the author is trying to communicate through this picture?

Students work silently, only moving on after each group member is ready. I believe this intra-personal time is important, because the next day each student is to become a tour guide for the rest of the class, and each student group will be responsible for guiding us around a small piece of the United States. Before then, however, students need to gain some *Flag: An American Story* expertise!

For the final five minutes of the first lesson, the students in each group decide on three photographs that they think represent three important and different aspects of America. Each student will be responsible for presenting and explaining one of the photographs, so all three group members need to have input into the photographs chosen. They write down their choices, which I collect, so that I can scan the selected pictures into my SMART Board software before the next day's lesson.

The next day, students spend the first ten minutes of the lesson preparing their segment of the tour. Each group member will present one photograph, a caption, and address the three questions used the day before. Students present a range of photographs, but two garner almost universal attention: (1) a photograph of a homeless, pregnant woman begging for money on a cold day, and (2) a photograph of a pastor seated in the doorway of his church.

The first photograph inspires feelings of pity, shame, guilt, and anger. The second photograph is eye-catching, but it is the caption that makes the picture the choice of so many students. The pastor in the photograph had written that each of us has our own mountain to climb, but no one can tell us how to climb it. Students think the caption shows two sides of America's troubles: Obstacles block our paths at certain points in our lives, but there are ways to climb over these obstacles. We just have to find them. The pastor's note acknowledges that although life in the United States is not perfect, happiness can still be found.

When we have completed our tour of Lauri Lyons' America, I tell the students that the next day we will be going on a tour. We will take a walking tour of the school and the school grounds with a camera and a five-foot tall American flag in tow. Students can work individually, in pairs, or in groups of three. They need to choose where they want to be photographed with the flag and decide how they will hold the flag. Their photographs will need to communicate their own vision or view of America. They will also have to write a short message to go with their photograph. Once all the pictures are taken, we can create our own American flag book, using the publishing opportunities on <www.lulu.com>.

The next day, I lead the students around the school, stopping whenever a student or group of students wants to take a photograph. Many interesting pictures are taken. I have two favorite pictures. In one, Benji and Alex are posing with the flag in the Lost and Found Box. To them, their photograph represents a country that occasionally loses its way and makes mistakes, but it is a country that always manages to find the correct path in the end. In the other, Brittany directs an interesting photograph that includes the entire class. She is sitting behind some railings, looking as if she is imprisoned, while the rest of the class marches toward her holding the American flag (see figure 4.3). Significantly, they are on the opposite side of the railings and not imprisoned at all. Her explanation of her photograph is poignant: Her family is part Native American, and her photograph represents the enclosure of Native American communities on reservations away from the rest of America. The class represents the Americans who walk by without so much as a glance in the direction of Native American hardships.

Figure 4.3 Brittany's photograph examines American attitudes toward Native American hardships.

I am impressed by the students' quality and depth of thought. Whenever I participate in student-constructed tours, I gain valuable insights of who my students are and learn about their dreams and hardships. I am grateful to the students for this experience and for their honesty.

Stephanie's Text-User Lessons

Instructional Disposition	Text User	Teaching Examples	Examples of Students' Work
Writing Practices	Uses knowledge to understand and shape writing by selecting different alternatives to fit social and academic situations	Having explored Lauri Lyons' photographs, I set a text creation task: Students are required to create their own photographic text and write a short message to explain their point of view.	Class takes a tour of the school, and groups of students organize photographs that portray their understanding and perception of America. Collected work is presented in a book published using www.lulu.com.
Discussion Across Texts	Participates in social and academic talk to differentiate and identify the purposes, uses, and contexts of different text forms	I orchestrate and initiate several discussions. Discussion takes place in a whole-class forum first of all, then in groups chosen by the teacher, and, lastly, in groups chosen by the students themselves.	• Whole-class discussion focuses on the contexts and the messages of two photographic texts. • Group discussions focus on choosing three photographs for each group's part of the tour. • Each student presents his or her part of the tour. • Groups decide where their photographs with the flag will take place and organize each picture.
Vocabulary	Recognizes and uses vocabulary for different purposes and contexts	I recall the relevant code breaker to represent his or her ideas. I emphasize explicitly the technical words; example: *close-up, medium shot, long shot.*	• Code-breaking students discuss the details that other students should look for when reading the photographs. • Technical language is explained. • Students use correct vocabulary when discussing and giving the tour of the photographs.
Intertextual Connections	Recognizes the construction and shapes of different meanings within and across text forms	I explain the two levels of touring the students will be doing: (1) exploring each photograph and message, then (2) reading across the photographs to establish the larger meaning and purpose of the book.	• Students participate in the reading of photographs – a new text type. • Students compare the photograph with the messages written by the participants in Lauri Lyons' book. • Students identify and present the range of meanings and interpretations of America by guiding the rest of the class through three photographs.
Engagement	Actively participates in using background knowledge to inquire about and use different text forms	I actively participate in the whole-class discussion on the opening two photographs.	• Students actively build meaning from the images through group work and discussion. • Students are engaged in the creation of their own photograph texts.
Reading Practices	Develops identities that use, analyze, and compare the way texts are shaped by intent and contexts	I clearly explain the role of text user and make sure that students know what to look for when interpreting a photograph. The questions I pose to the students require students to think about author purpose.	• Students act as tour guides, leading other students in the class around three of the photographs in the book. • Students learn that a text is more than just words – image can communicate just as strongly. • Students use their own background knowledge and experiences to create their own photograph texts.

Figure 4.4 This chart shows how all of the instructional dispositions are integrated into Stephanie's text-user lesson plans.

© 2010 Strop and Carlson

Lesson Aims	Lesson Sequence Details
I want my students to: • Understand how to create meaning, using image-based texts • Understand the role of the reader as tour guide • Verbally discuss and present ideas about these texts to the rest of the class • Create their own visual text and written comment	1. I introduce and explain the concept of the reader as tour guide. 2. I introduce *Flag: An American Story* and explain the layout and concept of the book. 3. I ask the students to nominate the code-breaker groups they would like to re-present their ideas. 4. The relevant code-breaker groups give advice on how to read an image-based text. I explain any technical vocabulary missed by the students: different kinds of shots, framing. 5. One at a time, I display two scanned photographs from the book on the SMART Board. I provide students with three guiding questions: (1) What do you notice? (2) What information can you glean about the people in the photograph? (3) What do you think the author is trying to communicate through this picture? 6. I give students some time to think about each image, and then invite them to volunteer their ideas and thoughts on the photograph. I ask: Can we, like archaeologists with artifacts, survey the photographs to piece together a meaning or story or message? 7. I ask students to predict what other pictures they might see in the book. I ask: What do you think is the connecting theme between pictures or the author's overall purpose? 8. Students spend 20 minutes reading text in silence, keeping note of their thoughts and reactions. The guiding questions remain on the board to scaffold students' thinking. 9. In groups of three, students decide on three photographs that really stand out to them and that represent three different aspects of America. They design a short tour of each photograph, making sure that the guiding questions are answered. Each student must present a text. 10. Groups present their sequence of three photographs. 11. Individually, students reflect on the photograph that stood out to them the most. Did any of the presentations influence their decision? 12. Students create their own photographic text by directing a shot containing either themselves or other members of the class posing with the American flag. 13. Students go to www.lulu.com to create a class version of *Flag: An American Story*.

Figure 4.5 Stephanie's text-user lesson plans – at a glance

Text Type	Linguistic (oral/written language)	Visual (still/moving images)	Auditory (music/sound)	Gestural (facial expression/body language)	Spatial (layout/organization of objects in space)
Photographs from *Flag: An American Story* by Lauri Lyons	Some photographs have wording featured in the image; example: the sign belonging to the homeless woman	Photographs – students need to focus on the flag, the subjects, and the background details	N/A	Some of the people in the photograph can be analyzed in terms of gesture, body language, and facial expression	The arrangement of the subjects and other objects within the photograph
Prose messages written by the participants in Lyons' project	Text that includes sometimes colorful vocabulary and interesting language	Some messages include doodles or brief drawings; handwriting can also be analyzed	N/A	N/A	N/A

Figure 4.6 Stephanie's text selections for her text-user lessons

Adapted from Anstey and Bull 2006

Text Type	Semiotic System	Genre	Learning Purpose	What Students Need to Know	What Students Need to Be Able to Do
Photographs from *Flag: An American Story* by Lauri Lyons Prose messages written by the participants in Lyons' project	Linguistic Visual Gestural Spatial Linguistic Visual	Visual nonfiction Personal nonfiction	• Understand how to create meaning using image-based texts • Understand the role of the reader as tour guide • Verbally discuss and present ideas about these texts to the rest of the class • Create own visual text	• How to code-break this text type – different kinds of shots, foreground and background details, lighting, color, framing, etc. • How to tour within and across texts • How to use background knowledge and personal experiences to bring texts to life • How to use own personal experiences and background knowledge to create texts	• Read the photographs, and establish a meaning and an authorial message and purpose • Understand that each reader may perceive the meaning differently • Take other students on a tour of three chosen photographs, highlighting the meaning (according to them), the message of the participants, and the message of the author • Use their own background and knowledge and experiences to create their own meaning via photography and writing

Adapted from Anstey and Bull 2006

Figure 4.7 Stephanie's text analysis for her text-user lessons

*   *   *

Stephanie described how her students became text users. She provided them with a map that showed them how to draw on other practices (code breaking and meaning making) and use the practices to deconstruct a photograph. Students applied their knowledge and skill by analyzing and interpreting a new visual text of their own creation. The students demonstrated their ability to design, create, put into action, and disseminate their own work. Like tour guides, the students became the leaders in their own academic learning and developed critical comprehension. They began to lead Stephanie and their classmates through the process of meaning making and of interpreting newly created texts.

Holly: Gatsby and the American Dream Unit

While students were building skills in code breaking and making meaning, they remained focused on the American Dream through the form and themes of *The Great Gatsby* and MTS that focused on the "new immigrants."

Now, students are ready to take a guided tour through MTS outside of *The Great Gatsby* in search of a character who engages them in a deeper understanding of the many facets of the American Dream. They will act as tour guides as they travel the same paths as the characters in the film and novels do. As their tours evolve, so do their levels of empathy for the array of American Dreamers they encounter.

To examine the way two types of texts are designed for different audiences and for potentially different purposes, students view the 2002[1] remake of *The Great Gatsby* story in the film *G*. This film portrays hip-hop artist "Summer G's" rise to fame, all the while still longing for his lost love. Students travel into the future (or back to the future?) to examine how the Gatsby story lives on in a different social context and how Summer G's rise to power is unique.

At this point in the unit, I invite students to tour a different context for the American Dream – the new immigrants and the evolving power hierarchies that define their status. As students view the film *G*, they step into the shoes of new immigrants who have come to the United States voluntarily and those who have come to America involuntarily. It is this second group of immigrants who often live as "caste minorities." I, therefore, ask students the following three discussion questions after we watch *G*:

1. How do race, lifestyle, and socioeconomic status reflect the levels of power among the black characters?
2. Are the main characters new immigrants, first- or second-generation immigrants, caste minorities, or others?
3. How do hope, wealth, and getting the partner shape a character's struggles for the American Dream?

After this discussion, we add to the graphic organizer (see figure 4.8) to help us visualize how perspectives on the unit's essential questions lead us to compare *G* to both the novel and the film of *The Great Gatsby*. I introduce the following questions to help students structure this comparison:

1. How does the filmmaker of *G* reinvent the characters in and story of *The Great Gatsby*?
2. By examining how elements of the American Dream manifest themselves in *G*, what do you learn about the filmmaker's purpose for making the movie?

---

1. The DVD was released in 2005.

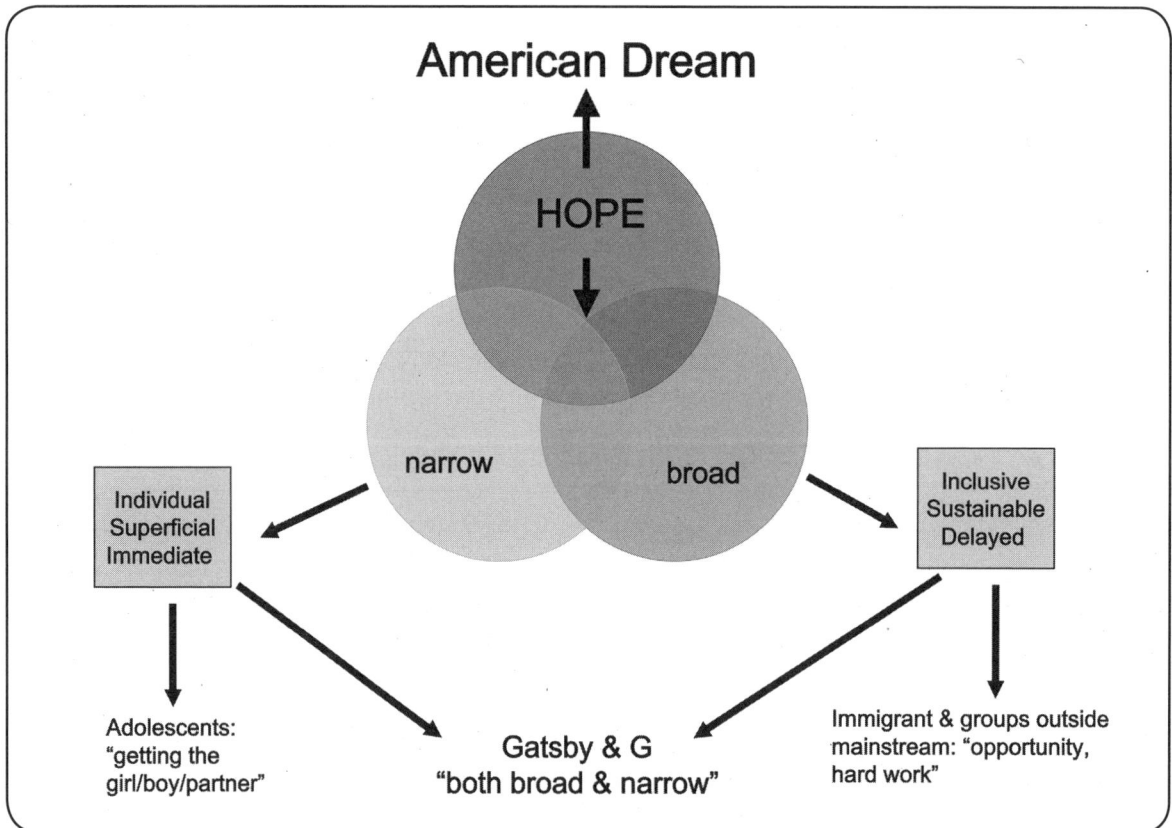

American Dream

HOPE

narrow   broad

Individual
Superficial
Immediate

Inclusive
Sustainable
Delayed

Adolescents:
"getting the
girl/boy/partner"

Gatsby & G
"both broad & narrow"

Immigrant & groups outside
mainstream: "opportunity,
hard work"

Figure 4.8 Students revisit the graphic organizer.

Next, I invite students to journey into the lives of several other characters and to examine other routes to the American Dream. To accomplish this, I divide the class into several groups. I assign one of the following books to each group: An Na's *Wait for Me*, Sherman Alexie's *The Absolutely True Diary of a Part-Time Indian*, or Markus Zusak's *Getting the Girl*. As their reading progresses, students alternate between discussions conducted with same-title groups and discussions with those from other-title groups. I direct them to return to the same questions examined during our discussion of *G*.

We also take time to watch the film *The Namesake* (2006)[2]. Again, students literally travel the path of someone new: an adult immigrant to the United States from India. Students respond to this informal writing prompt: "How does your reaction to Ashoke and Ashima's search for the American Dream differ from your reaction to the search by Gatsby, Summer G, Mina, Junior, and Ruben?" The graphic organizer (see figure 4.8) is displayed as students respond in writing. Students can opt to use the organizer as a guide.

---

2. The DVD was released in 2007.

As a cumulative experience, students choose or are assigned a character from the novel they have read in their small groups. To develop a character "profile," students use the American Dream Panel Interview Planning Guide (see BLM 8, appendix B). After this, I lead the class in brainstorming a list of "interview questions." These questions help students bridge the time periods, cultures, social contexts, and power hierarchies represented in the MTS. Students will use the questions to guide interviews of characters from all the novels and films covered in this unit.

Following the tour-guide frame, students prepare answers to questions from the perspective of their chosen or assigned characters (one from *Gatsby* and one from any of the other texts). Students "travel" on "An MTS Tour of the American Dream." The interviewees visit the "Land of Wealth," "Land of Hope," or "Land of Getting/Keeping the Partner." The interview requires students to respond to questions posed by student interviewers (tour guides) who travel to each "land," trying to gain greater insight into the American Dream. I work with each student who is acting as a tour guide. I help these students structure and categorize the questions they plan to ask. Before the interview, those being interviewed are provided with the questions they will be asked. These students then have the opportunity to extract specific examples and quotes from texts to substantiate their responses. They are also encouraged to interact with the interviewers and with each other (whether prompted by the interviewers, or not).

Holly's Text-User Lessons

Instructional Disposition	Text User	Teaching Examples	Examples of Students' Work
Writing Practices	Uses knowledge to understand and shape writing by selecting different alternatives to fit social and academic situations	• I provide a format for students to compare their impressions of the similarities and differences between various literary and film characters' quests for the American Dream (AD). • After soliciting sample questions from the class as a whole, I model the type of questions that could be asked. I work with those who are acting as tour guides to structure, write, and share the questions for each "Land."	• Students respond to an informal writing prompt after they view *The Namesake*. • Students write answers to questions they anticipate the interviewer/tour guide will ask as the tour moves from the Land of Wealth to the Land of Getting/Keeping the Partner to the Land of Hope.
Discussion Across Texts	Participates in social and academic talk to differentiate and identify the purposes, uses, and contexts of different text forms	I organize Book Club discussion groups that alternate between same-title groups and mixed-title groups. We use the questions from *G* to launch discussion.	In Book Club style discussions, students use their knowledge of different narratives and characters in both books and film to connect to the essential questions tied to the AD.
Vocabulary	Recognizes and uses vocabulary for different purposes and contexts	I help students draw parallels between characters in our new texts and *Gatsby* by clarifying the terms *cultural contexts, social contexts, power hierarchies, new immigrants, voluntary immigrants,* and *caste minorities*.	Students use the terms *cultural contexts, social contexts, power hierarchies, new immigrants, voluntary immigrants,* and *caste minorities* as they ask and answer questions on the Tour.
Intertextual Connections	Recognizes the construction and shapes of different meanings within and across text forms	• Students read "new immigrant" novels to explore the perspectives of the adolescent protagonists and their quests for the AD. We view *The Namesake* to focus on voluntary immigrants and their ADs. • For the "MTS Tour," I encourage student choice for one role and appoint students to their second roles.	For the "MTS Tour," students take on multiple roles, one from *Gatsby* and one from a film or Book Club text.
Engagement	Actively participates in using background knowledge to inquire about and use different text forms	I show the hip-hop culture film *G* and prompt students to look for how major characters have "modernized" Fitzgerald's novel.	Students view *G* through two lenses: (1) How does the filmmaker reinvent the *Gatsby* characters and story? (2) By examining how elements of the AD manifest themselves, what do we learn about the filmmaker's purpose?
Reading Practices	Develops identities that use, analyze, and compare the way texts are shaped by intent and contexts	I assist students in choosing textual support specific to the characters they represent. Students examine whether their characters are succeeding or failing in the pursuit of their ADs, as evaluated through their attainment of wealth, capacities for hope, and abilities to get/keep the partner.	Students read for different purposes to prepare to ask and answer questions as part of the "MTS Tour" (AD Panel Interview).

Figure 4.9 This chart shows how all of the instructional dispositions are integrated into Holly's text-user lessons.

Lesson Aims	Lesson Sequence Details
I want my students to: • Understand the role of the reader as tour guide • Connect and compare ideas from multiple texts using academic talk • Verbally discuss, present, and support ideas • Draw from background knowledge to use different texts to communicate different perspectives	1. In order to establish background knowledge for students, I present a short lesson on the "new immigrants" and clarify terms such as *first/second generation immigrant, caste minority*, etc. 2. Students view the hip-hop culture film *G* to determine how the filmmaker has reinvented the *Gatsby* story and to examine the filmmaker's purpose related to the American Dream (AD). 3. I lead a discussion on factors that empower the black characters, how they fit any "immigrant" labels, and how hope, wealth, and getting the partner shape their struggles. 4. We bring our observations together as we revisit and add to our "cumulative" graphic organizer. 5. Students are placed in heterogeneous groups to read YA new immigrant novels. Next, in book-alike and mixed groups, they discuss the questions used to analyze *G*. 6. Students view the film *The Namesake* and complete a writing prompt that used the "cumulative" graphic organizer as a springboard for comparing the ADs of adult immigrants with those of teen immigrants.

Figure 4.10 Holly's text-user lesson plans – at a glance

Text Type	Linguistic (oral/written language)	Visual (still/moving images)	Auditory (music/sound)	Gestural (facial expression/body language)	Spatial (layout/organization of objects in space)
Novel	Prose, dialogue, vocabulary, style	Book cover	N/A	N/A	N/A
Film	Dialogue, tone, volume, pitch, rate, dialect	DVD cover	Sound effects, music	Actors' expressions and movements	Actors' distance from each other ("social bubbles")

Adapted from Anstey and Bull 2006

Figure 4.11 Holly's text selections for her text-user lessons

Text Type	Semiotic System	Genre	Learning Purpose	What Students Need to Know	What Students Need to Be Able to Do
Novel	Linguistic	Fiction	• To understand how the essential questions can be formulated as questions to be asked of characters from the MTS • To understand how the American Dream (AD) is pursued by multiple characters from different perspectives and life experiences in order to role-play those characters in a panel interview	• The terms *cultural contexts, social contexts, power hierarchies, new immigrants, voluntary immigrants,* and *caste minorities* • Through the use of the unit's graphic organizer, Gatsby represents a "baseline" for comparison to all other texts in the MTS	• Read for purpose, and analyze multiple characters' level of attainment of the AD • Participate in panel interviews as characters from several texts in the MTS, focusing on wealth, hope, and getting/keeping the partner
Film	Linguistic Visual Auditory Gestural Spatial	Fiction	• To understand how the AD is pursued by a new "voluntary immigrant" of adult status	• How the elements of the film portray the elements of the AD	• Discuss the filmmaker's purpose • Write about their impressions of the characters as they compare to others in the MTS

Adapted from Anstey and Bull 2006

Figure 4.12 Holly's text analysis for her text-user lessons

*   *   *

Holly expertly guided the students to read, view, and interpret multiple perspectives of the characters in each of the texts. Like tour guides, the students took the lead and role-played both interviewer and interviewee. Holly supported students in writing to learn and, ultimately, in analyzing film, filmmakers, story characters, and era. She continued to build upon the code breaker and meaning maker to direct students into deeper comprehension of this MTS.

Richard: Vietnam War Unit

The two seminal, and central, texts of the Vietnam unit are Greg Vistica's cover story for *The New York Times Magazine*, "One Awful Night in Thanh Phong," and the CBS *60 Minutes II* video segment, "Memories of a Massacre." These are two versions of the same story, written and produced by some of the same people, yet they are separate texts, designed for different audiences and for, arguably, different purposes. In the role of athlete, my students practiced code breaking various semiotic systems by recognizing their structural conventions and patterns. As archaeologists, they had opportunities to contextualize the information from additional brief texts. Now, I challenge them to become tour guides for the two abovementioned central texts by putting together their previous unit activities as a text user. Because these texts are quite similar (but not identical) in their story, but distinctly different in their structure, the texts provide a rich opportunity for my students to note how form shapes the meaning of a text.

I ask my students to read the print piece first. I am not certain that giving them the print text first makes any difference in their skill acquisition, but it helps to provide an incentive for reading when they know that the next text will be a video. To their minds, video is a typically "easier" type of text to understand! As with previous lessons in this unit, we consider the specific vocabulary of Vistica's essay. I provide students with a handout of words from the text that may prove challenging. Some of the words are general-usage vocabulary, some are Vietnam War specific (for example, *charismatic, vagaries, pro forma, hootches, LAWs*). As the students read, I ask them to provide working definitions of the words from any context clues they note. They then use a dictionary to find and jot down essential definitions for each challenging word.

This text also contains photographs that are used to illustrate the story and generate additional meaning and knowledge. Students actively read this story, using sticky notes to mark interesting sites on this "tour." After reading, students complete Part A of the worksheet (see figure 4.13) to compare the ideas and stories of the primary characters, Bob Kerrey and Gerhard Klann.

I direct the students to consider the authorial purposes of this text, and to consider the various audiences for whom it was created. I point out that Gregory Vistica did not likely have a captive audience of junior and senior high-school students in mind as his primary audience. Why does this text exist – what is the author's intention? What purpose does it serve? What are its codes and conventions, and how do these elements of its form shape its meanings? What information seems key and essential? What information seems to be missing or may have been edited out? I ask students which of the two main characters, Kerrey or Klann, seems more sympathetic. Many side with Bob Kerrey.

Name: _____ Hr: _____

Whom Do You Believe?

In the table below, indicate the similarities in and differences between the stories told by Bob Kerrey and Gerhard Klann for the night of February 25, 1969. Use Greg Vistica's article, "One Awful Night in Thanh Phong" to complete Table 1. Use the CBS video, "Memories of a Massacre," to complete Table 2.

As you work, consider these questions:

- What is being compared (alike) and what is being contrasted (different)?
- What categories of characteristics or attributes are used to compare and contrast these things?
- How are the things alike or similar?
- How are the things not alike or different?
- What are the most important qualities or attributes that make them similar?
- What are the most important qualities or attributes that make them different?
- In terms of the qualities that are most important, are these things more alike or more different?
- What can we conclude about these things?

Part A
Table 1: One Awful Night in Thanh Phong

Compared Ideas	Circle "A for alike; "D" for different	Bob Kerrey Page #	Gerhard Klann Page #
	A D		
	A D		
	A D		
	A D		
	A D		
	A D		
	A D		
	A D		

Figure 4.13 Worksheet, Part A

Part B
Table 2: Memories of a Massacre

Compared Ideas	Circle "A for alike; "D" for different	Bob Kerrey Page #	Gerhard Klann Page #
	A D		
	A D		
	A D		
	A D		
	A D		
	A D		
	A D		
	A D		

Figure 4.13 (cont'd): Worksheet, Part B

I ask students whose story they believe more fully, Kerry's or Klann's? Why? What elements of the medium (magazine text) lead them to their conclusions? I have them consider codes, conventions, author's intention, and what has been left out.

After some class discussion of the text, notes made by students, and the graphic organizer, we view the video, "Memories of a Massacre," from CBS *60 Minutes II*. Because we "read" video at essentially the same rate – the rate controlled by the producer – we watch the video together as a class. I encourage students to ask questions or make comments as necessary. I control the remote and pause or rewind at propitious or confusing parts of the text. After the viewing, students complete Part B of the worksheet (see figure 4.13). I again ask questions regarding authorial intent and the ways in which this text makes its meanings. In part, because we see and hear a moderator, Dan Rather, asking questions in the conventional manner of a *60 Minutes* interview, the students often express a preference for this text. As a result, students generally make quicker and more particular inferences about the characters and events in the story based on Rather's questions, the uses of the cameras and editing techniques, and lighting conventions.

The juxtaposition of these two texts invariably generates an enthusiastic discussion, fueled by the various similarities and contrasts the students have noted in their graphic organizers. It is at this point that many students, operating as independent tour guides, become aware of the many distinctive facets of the "tour" and the different contexts of the experience of the text. It is also when some students, putting into play all their practice and knowledge of the how texts are consumed, have epiphanies about the text in terms of its purpose and meaning.

This directed comparison allows me to lead students back to the essential questions with which we began our unit:

1. How do media affect our interpretation of a news story?
2. How do multiple perspectives (e.g., different media) shape our perception of the truth?
3. What constitutes a war crime?

Richard's Text-User Lessons

Instructional Disposition	Text User	Teaching Examples	Examples of Students' Work
Writing Practices	Uses knowledge to understand and shape writing by selecting different alternatives to fit social and academic situations	I offer students graphic organizer to help them classify information from the texts and to better see the patterns the text reveals.	Students respond to the short answers at the end of the graphic organizer for "Memories of a Massacre."
Discussion Across Texts	Participates in social and academic talk to differentiate and identify the purposes, uses, and contexts of different text forms	I use the graphic organizer to promote specific examples from the text, to compare patterns in the text, to contrast ideas in the text.	Because there is room for distinctive inferences and students overlay the texts with their own values and biases, they are eager to offer their conclusions about these two texts.
Vocabulary	Recognizes and uses vocabulary for different purposes and contexts	Again, we collect vocabulary for our word wall, and both my students and I employ new words in our writing and discussions.	Again, we collect vocabulary for our word wall, and both I and my students employ new words in our writing and discussions.
Intertextual Connections	Recognizes the construction and shapes of different meanings within and across text forms	I sometimes "prime the pump" of connection making by offering disparate pieces of information from these two texts.	Students tend to work reinforce their inferences or made meanings during discussions by referencing, sometimes doggedly, the two texts.
Engagement	Actively participates in using background knowledge to inquire about and use different text forms	I ask how students' background knowledge helps them to feel more "expert" in terms of the ideas and positions of these two texts.	Students demonstrate facile connections between what they knew coming in to the unit and what they have learned through the MTS study of this unit.
Reading Practices	Develops identities that use, analyze, and compare the way texts are shaped by intent and contexts	Again, I model distinctions between the Vistica print text and the Vistica-produced video text in order to promote distinctions from the students themselves.	Students often will preface their comments by suggesting authorial intent.

© 2010 Strop and Carlson

Figure 4.14 This chart shows how all of the instructional dispositions are integrated into Richard's text-user lessons.

Lesson Aims	Lesson Sequence Details
I want my students to: • Activate prior knowledge and lessons • Understand the role of the reader as a user of texts, using the metaphor of a tour guide • Develop a stance of empowerment as readers by understanding the distinctive contextual bases of various texts • Assess how contexts and technical features of texts influence how and what a reader does with them	1. I remind students of the prior knowledge of the Vietnam War and the vocabulary, texts, and essential questions of the unit. 2. I present the "tour guide" metaphor to students. 3. I distribute reprints of journalist Greg Vistica's "One Awful Night in Thanh Phong," along with a list of challenging vocabulary and blank sticky notes. 4. I instruct students to actively read this text, using the sticky notes to mark interesting, significant, or unclear sections of the story (the several photographs used to illustrate Vistica's story must also be included in their thinking). In addition, I remind them to provide working definitions for the vocabulary words based on context clues or to look them up in their dictionaries. 5. After reading, I ask students to use a graphic organizer to highlight the similarities and the differences between the two principle characters and their accounts of that "awful night in Thanh Phong." After processing time, we report out. Patterns emerge and discrepancies are noted. 6. Noting the media triangle graphic on the front board, I direct the students to consider the authorial purposes of this text, and to consider the various audiences for whom it was created. I am quick to point out that Gregory Vistica did not likely have a captive audience of junior and senior high-school students in mind as his primary audience. Given that, why does this text exist? What purpose does it serve? What are its codes and conventions, and how do these elements of its form shape its meanings? What information that was included seems key and essential? What information seems missing or may have been edited out? I ask students which of the two main characters, Kerrey or Klann, seems more sympathetic? Discussion ensues. 7. We view the CBS *60 Minutes II* videotext, "Memories of a Massacre." This time, I ask students to complete the graphic organizer for comparison of characters, ideas, and codes and conventions as they view the video. I provide ample opportunity for reviewing portions of the tape and pausing for questions or clarifications. 8. At the conclusion of our viewing, I ask students to provide thoughtful, brief responses to the questions at the end of the graphic organizer. 9. I invite students to share their thoughts on both versions of this same story – the print/photo text and the video/audio text. They naturally compare both the distinctive characteristics and contexts of each text as well as the content of each, and are led to some conclusions about each.

Figure 4.15 Richard's text-user lesson plans – at a glance

Text Type	Linguistic (oral/written language)	Visual (still/moving images)	Auditory (music/sound)	Gestural (facial expression/body language)	Spatial (layout/organization of objects in space)
Prose nonfiction: "One Awful Night at Thanh Phong," an historical narrative Photographs: various images of Bob Kerrey and his fellow Navy Seals from the Vietnam War and Vietnam landscapes Video/audio tape: "Memories of a Massacre"	All prose texts contain words in various syntactic patterns; some contain Arabic numerals N/A Dialogue, narration, volume, tone, pitch, rate, dialect	N/A Navy Seal images; Vietnamese geographical imagery Video footage; various codes and conventions (camera angles, shots, lighting, color, etc.), focal points of imagery	N/A Voices of interviews, music, sound effects	N/A Present in images of Navy Seals Various expressions of body language and attitudes of the people in the photos Expressions and body language of interviewers and interviewees	N/A Positions of persons in the photos; foreground, middle ground, background Codes and conventions: camera shots

Figure 4.16 Richard's text selections for his text-user lessons

Adapted from Anstey and Bull 2006

Text Type	Semiotic System	Genre	Learning Purpose	What Students Need to Know	What Students Need to Be Able to Do
Prose: Narrative nonfiction Videotape Still images	Linguistic Visual Visual Auditory Visual Gestural Spatial	Prose Nonfiction historical narrative Photography	• Engage their own knowledge, skill sets, and patterns of practice as readers of text • Recognize familiar and obvious patterns, codes, meanings • Identify or synthesize new or different ideas, patterns, or meanings in the text	To assess how contexts and technical features of texts influence how and what a reader does with them	Develop a stance of empowerment as readers by understanding the distinctive contextual bases of various texts

Figure 4.17 Richard's text analysis for his text-user lessons

Adapted from Anstey and Bull 2006

* * *

Richard showed how to juxtapose and read two versions of the same event and discuss the similarities and differences in each context. He clearly demonstrated the elements of the lesson: (1) how background knowledge is built to prepare students for the next step, and (2) how students become independent tour guides by reading, analyzing, and engaging in the different genre. Like tour guides, the students then became their own guides by directing themselves through diverse contexts and literacy experiences.

PLANNING FOR THE TEXT-USER ROLE

In this chapter, the lessons modeled how to prepare and encourage students to become independent readers and thinkers as they navigated through challenging texts. There were examples of independent practice and group-idea exchanges where the text users decimated meanings and purposes for certain styles of texts such as powerful images (both still and film), as well as comics. (See BLM 7, appendix B.)

The questions we asked you to consider at the beginning of this chapter are listed again. Examine and apply the questions to your own planning of a text-user lesson within MTS. After you have drafted your text-user lesson, use the planning chart to analyze it (see BLM 2, appendix B).

While reading and analyzing each of the lessons, think about or ask yourself the following questions:

1. How are my students thinking like tour guides and using texts?
2. How do I plan to support and encourage students to maintain and effectively use this role in their learning and monitoring?
3. Where will I integrate this role in my own practice?

Chapter 5

Film Reviewer as Text Critic

*Successful literacy programs might make one just literate enough to get in real trouble...
to be ideologically deceived...An alternative to the conventional approaches of identifying
bias and stereotypes...focus students' views of texts both on technical detail and on social
context...speculate on what kind of person, in what kind of cultural or historical context,
might have written such a text...focus on how a text might indeed construct its ideal reader...
focus on "what a text is trying to do to me" opens up discussions of the intention, force, and
effects of texts upon particular audiences (Luke 2000, 455).*

*Analyze and transform text by acting on knowledge that texts are not ideologically
natural or neutral – that they represent particular points of views while silencing others
and influence people's ideas – and that their designs and discourses can be critiqued
and redesigned in novel and hybrid ways (Luke and Freebody 1999, 5).*

Luke and Freebody (1999) explain the role of text critic as a process of breaking the
code, making meaning, considering the uses of the text, and then acting on that
knowledge with a critical eye. The text critic, recognizing that texts have multiple
points of view, asks the following four questions:

1. Who is being represented and influenced?
2. How can this text be viewed from a different perspective?
3. What are the preferred and oppositional readings?
4. Who wrote and produced this text?

If you learn and use code-breaking skills to deconstruct a political cartoon, for
example, you would consider the elements (print and visual) within each frame and
then the overall design of the elements as a whole. By deciding what story is being told
or what message is being communicated – through tone and language (both words
and images) – you would make meaning.

As you consider the use of a political cartoon, you also consider the context and form:

1. In what context did the cartoon get published?
2. Who created the cartoon?
3. Was it published in a newspaper or online?
4. When was it created?

After you bring all of these literacy practices together, you decide upon and question
which points of view are represented and which are absent. We discuss these and

decide how and why it is important to note these perspectives. Students learn to recognize voice and power within visuals and print.

When we introduce students to the role of text critic, we use the metaphor of *film reviewer* as text critic. This metaphor helps the students think about the purposes, skills, and context necessary to this role. The role of a film reviewer who writes for a newspaper, magazine, TV, or online site is to provide information about films. Readers use this information to help them decide whether or not to see the film. Reviewers also have the writing skills and film knowledge to help viewers appreciate the art of film making and/or the potential impact of the film as a catalyst for change. Film reviewers need to know about film genres, literature, and how films are made (including writing, acting, and production). The reviewer also has to be aware of the audience he or she is writing for. These are some of the questions that a film reviewer asks:

- Who are the viewers I am trying to influence or inform?

- What aspects of this film should I feature in my review?

- What criteria should I use that will speak to my intended audience?

- How should I communicate my review?

- What language should I use to be sure I do not "talk down" to my audience?

- What influences do my own experiences, knowledge, and preferences have on my response to the film?

- What other films or literature can I refer to so the reader can make intertextual connections to support his or her decision-making process?

- What does my publisher expect me to communicate to its audience?

- What forms of language are common in this publication?

Thus, for students to be effective text critics, they need to develop a disposition of a film reviewer that combines the resources and knowledge needed from all four roles: code breaker, meaning maker, text user, and text critic (Anstey and Bull 2006). As students practice the role of text critic, their personal responses and critical perspectives fuel their thinking. This leads to the kind of divergent thinking that eventually spirals into engagement.

In this chapter, we present classroom examples of practicing the role of text critic by "reviewing" texts within MTS. The text critic portions of figure 1.3 and figure 1.5, which compare instructional dispositions and literacy practices, are reprinted here for you to refer to as you follow the classroom lessons (see figure 5.1 and figure 5.2).

TEXT CRITIC IN PRACTICE

As text critic, the student's frame of mind should be that of a film reviewer who informs and influences readers' viewing choices while maintaining the goals of the publication he or she is writing for.

Instructional Disposition	Text Critic
Writing Practices	Uses awareness of writing strategies, intertextuality, and text design to influence different audiences and interest groups
Discussion Across Texts	Participates in social and academic talk to understand, critique, or debate various perspectives within and across a set of texts
Vocabulary	Recognizes and analyzes the ways that language and vocabulary influence readers, listeners, and viewers
Intertextual Connections	Recognizes and assumes that texts are not neutral, and explores the perspectives within and across texts
Engagement	Actively participates in analyzing, critiquing, and questioning texts from different perspectives as reader, viewer, or listener
Reading Practices	Develops identities that develop an expectation that considers different meanings and perspectives constructed and produced to elicit particular responses

Figure 5.1 This chart shows the intersection of the instructional dispositions and the literacy practice of text critic.

Role (description)	Practice (questions)	Scaffolds (literacy)	MTS (context)
Text critic (critical competence): Analyze and change meaning of texts by acting on the understanding of and critiquing of different points of view that can silence and influence	• What kind of person, with what interests and values, could both write and read this naively and unproblematically? • What is this text trying to do to me? In whose interests? • Which positions, voices, and interests are at play? Which are silent and absent?	Students are taught to second guess the conditions of text production and text reception. Teach students to consider preferred and oppositional readings and how texts are constructed and produced to bring about particular responses.	

Adapted from Luke 2000; Luke and Freebody 1999; Anstey and Bull 2006

Figure 5.2 The literacy practice of text critic in multimedia text sets. The right-hand column can be filled in with examples from the topic being studied.

The lesson plans that follow model how the role of text critic is practiced in different grade levels. Stephanie illustrates how text critic is practiced with seventh graders, Holly teaches high-school English, and Richard's work is in a high school media literacy class.

While reading and analyzing each lesson, think about or ask yourself the following three questions:

1. How are the students thinking like film reviewer and text critics?
2. How do I support and encourage students to maintain and effectively use this role in their learning and monitoring?
3. Where will I integrate this role in my own practice?

Stephanie: Americana Unit

When students take on the role of text critic, they assume a position of power – as language theorists such as Barthes (1967) and Rosenblatt (1968) point out, the reader is in control. Once a manuscript is out of the author's hand, it is at the mercy of the reader, and the reader will make whatever he or she wants to make of the text.

Sometimes, I believe, students forget that they are in control of the code-breaking and meaning-making processes. When they forget, they often become intimidated by complex texts and frustrated by attempts to figure out what an author means. When I teach students how to become text critics, I make them conscious of their dominant position in the author-reader-text triangle. Students, as text critics, have the ability to interpret and judge the text as they see fit. The meaning of any given text is out of the author's hands. Only the reader truly matters.

At this point in the Americana unit, students get to choose their reading text from a big box of books. Included in the box are poetry books, classic novels, young-adult fiction and nonfiction, cartoon strips, magazines, and graphic novels. I try to include as many different texts as possible on a variety of topics so that every student will find something he or she enjoys reading. I also encourage students to locate their own books, as long as the texts relate to the theme of Americana. Popular choices include The Clique series by Lisi Harrison, Eric Schlosser and Charles Wilson's *Chew on This* (which is the young-adult version of the authors' *Fast Food Nation*), S. E. Hinton's *The Outsiders*, and Mark Twain's *The Adventures of Huckleberry Finn*. I recommend to students that they read a book they like. If they find they are not enjoying the book, I tell them it is perfectly acceptable to switch to another book. They then spend two to three weeks reading the book and maintaining a reading journal. At the end of this reading period, they are ready to become text critics.

My text-critic activities require a sequence of lessons.

Lesson 1

I begin, as always, by talking about the role my students will be assuming. Since they will be taking on the role of text critic, I make the comparison between the film reviewer and the text critic. As a class, our first job is to think about the kinds of things a film reviewer writes about. I give students two film reviews written by film critic Roger Ebert (although movie reviews by other critics are perfectly acceptable). I like to use reviews that are of current movies to keep interest levels as high as possible. I also like the reviews to be of movies that have dissimilar target audiences. For example, one year I used the film reviews for *City of Ember* (PG) and *The Secret Life of Bees* (PG-13). The first movie is based on a popular young-adult book, while the second movie has a decidedly feminine appeal. After students have read the reviews, we compile a list of the things that Roger Ebert commented on or included in his review. The list that my first-quarter class compiled included:

- Brief summary of what happens – although the ending is not given away

- Description of the time period and setting

- Reference to genre; for example, *City of Ember* is referred to as a "Boys' and Girls' Own Adventure"

- Adjectives that describe the movie

- Description of our feelings toward the main characters

- References to other texts; for example, Roger Ebert compares one part of *The Secret Life of Bees* to the friendship and escape of Huck and Jim in Mark Twain's *Huckleberry Finn*

- Comments on cultural issues today; for example, Ebert comments on the lack of minority representation in *City of Ember*

- Judgments about whether the movie was good or bad

- Judgments about whether the movie was realistic or historically accurate

- References to other reviewers' opinions

- Comments about the audience for which each movie was created; for example, Ebert states that the movie *City of Ember* is "innocent" and aimed at younger viewers

- Questions that occur while watching the movie

- Grade or rating

After exploring the reviews and coming up with our list, students have some time to independently critique the book/text they have been reading. They share their critiques in mini-guides that they make (see BLM 9, appendix B).

Making a mini-guide:

1. Fold a piece of plain paper into four pieces.

2. Staple down the vertical fold.

3. Cut along the remaining horizontal fold (to create a small eight-page booklet).

Students create a text cover on the first page of the guide. The cover should not merely depict a scene from the text; it should bring together the important elements and themes that are in the book/text. The design should be symbolic, not literal. On page 2, students write an explanation of the cover. On pages 3–6, they write thoughtful responses to the following questions:

- Does your text remind you of any other text? (Remember a text is anything that communicates a message, for example, novel, poem, song, film, TV show.)

- Does your text remind you of any current issues happening in today's world? Explain your answer.

- What do you think was the author's purpose in writing the text you chose? Is there a message or moral for the reader?

- What kind of person or audience is your text written for? Do you fit into the intended audience? Does the intended audience of the text affect your enjoyment?

- What is your reaction to the text and the things that happened in it? Would other people with different lives, situations, and experiences react differently to your text?

- What are your text's good points? What changes or improvements could have been/ need to be made?

To help students with their books, I show them the mini-guide I made for *Bone by Bone by Bone*, a young-adult book by Tony Johnston. The story focuses on a young boy torn between the ideals of his white supremacist father and his loyalty to his African-American best friend.

First, I explain the reasoning and the symbolism behind my front cover, which is a skeleton set against a red background with black-and-white question marks labeling various bones. Next, I show my written answers to the questions I posed (see above). I focus on the author's message: racism is dangerously wrong, and I draw students' attention to a note by the author at the beginning of the book. Here, the author writes that she has been troubled her entire life by her father's racist ideals. This sentiment is also reflected in the book's dedication, which is to her father. The book, then, also becomes a message about fathers and daughters (even though the main character is a boy), parents and children. Both the note and the dedication add a meaning and a purpose that I would have missed without reading them. My personal reaction to the story is one of outrage and anger toward the father in the novel; but we do discuss how others might react. The class agrees that the majority of people would react the way I have reacted. However, one student talks about an episode of *Oprah* that featured a white supremacist family from the South. The student thinks that the family would agree with the father, not with the author.

I give students two class periods to work on their mini-guides. While they work on their guides, I make a ratings scale. I create a giant red line that stretches from the floor to almost the ceiling in the cafeteria near my room (no space inside my classroom). The top of the scale signifies excellence; the bottom of the line denotes the opposite. This is the only preparation I need to do for the next lesson, when I ask students to rate their text.

Lesson 2

This lesson begins with an introduction to the ratings scale. Students bring their mini-guides and their chairs into our new learning arena in the cafeteria. I explain that I want each student to come to the front and talk for a minute about the book he or she has read. I encourage them to use their mini-guide to help them with the content of their presentation. Each presentation ends with the presenter ceremoniously attaching, with a small wad of masking tape, his or her mini-guide to the ratings scale. If students place their mini-guide at the top of the scale, it means they really liked the book. If they place their mini-guide at the bottom of the scale, it means the book is one of the worst they have ever read. If they place the mini-guide right in the middle, they think the book is good but not great. I give students a few minutes to think over the content of their presentations and where they are going to rate their books. Students listen carefully to each presentation and make a note of any text that stands out to them as being really excellent and interesting

Students have, so far, worked on the text-critic role independently. However, I want to give my students the chance to critically discuss texts together, because the text critic does not operate in isolation but looks at a text from a variety of angles and positions. Students need to realize that recognizing and listening to others' responses are key parts of being a critic. Like the film reviewer, they do not work for themselves and by themselves, but for a potentially diverse audience with a range of priorities, interests, and points of view.

With this in mind, I divide the class into groups of three students and give them their first challenge: we are going to present an award to the best Americana text. The award is to be called the Meyer Middle School Medal for the Best Americana Text. We looked over the criteria for the Michael L. Printz Award for Excellence, an award given annually to a young-adult novel. After a brief discussion, each group then decides on three criteria they think the winning text needs to meet. We then collate the criteria on the SMART Board (see figure 5.3).

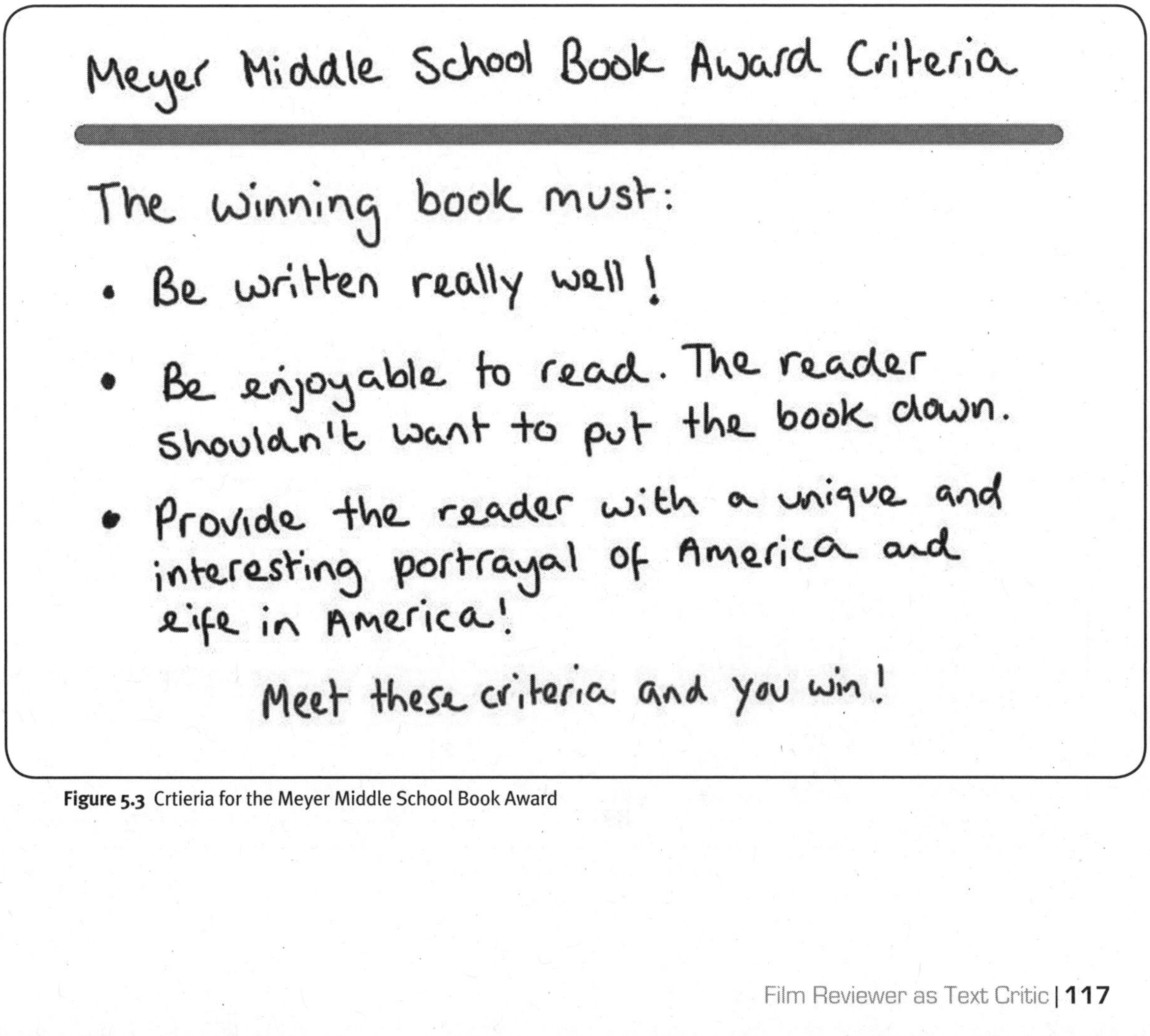

Meyer Middle School Book Award Criteria

The winning book must:

- Be written really well !

- Be enjoyable to read. The reader shouldn't want to put the book down.

- Provide the reader with a unique and interesting portrayal of America and life in America!

Meet these criteria and you win !

Figure 5.3 Crtieria for the Meyer Middle School Book Award

With the criteria for our award established, I ask each group to review their notes from the previous day's presentations and nominate *one* text for the award.

Lesson 3

Each group questions the students with the nominated texts about their texts. The questions and the answers help the students decide on a final winner. Each group gets one vote. Groups are then given time to think about the questions they would like to ask. As text critics, the students need to ask themselves: Do we now have the information we need to make an informed critical decision about which text gets the award? As the groups work and discuss suitable questions, the nominated students are allowed to listen to the discussions and take notes so that they know what kinds of questions they will be asked. I do not want students to feel intimidated by being put on the spot with no idea of what will be asked of them; that is not the point of the activity. The point of the question/answer session is for each voting group to gather information needed to make an informed decision (see figure 5.4).

The classroom is then transformed into a panel-discussion forum. Seats are set out at the front of the classroom for the students who have read the nominated books. These seats face the rest of the students, whose chairs have been placed in rows. Students are given 20 minutes to ask the nominees questions about their texts. Those in the audience make notes of the questions asked and the answers given. Questions can be

Meyer Middle School Book Award

Each entrant must be prepared to:

- Introduce the book
- Provide short plot summary
- Explain his or her connection to the book
- Explain what kind of readers will like the book
- Describe the portrayal of America as offered by the book
- Explain why this book represents "great literature"
- Read a paragraph that best represents the book.
- Answer any panel questions!!!

Figure 5.4 Each contestant is required to fulfill the criteria of the student panel

directed at the entire panel or to individual nominees. I also encourage students to deviate from their written list of questions if a question occurs to them spontaneously as a result of an answer given. I want them to dig deep.

Just as film reviewers select their favorites for picture of the year, my students now need to finalize their opinion on who should win our Americana text award. The last ten minutes of class are dedicated to deciding on a winner. Each group re-forms and students discuss the answers given during the panel session. They then have to decide on one winner and write a critical review of the text they select, explaining why it deserves to win. I remind students that while their text criticism should reflect their honest opinion, it is also a persuasive piece designed to make the audience feel the same way as they do about the text they have chosen to win. I also distribute copies of the Ebert reviews and show the list of critical elements constructed at the start of this lesson sequence. The students' reviews should contain similar information.

The nominations are tallied, a winner is announced. The student of the winning text is awarded the Meyer Middle School Medal for the Best Americana Text. During these lessons, my students have truly become text critics.

Stephanie's Text-Critic Lessons

Instructional Disposition	Text Critic	Teaching Examples	Examples of Students' Work
Writing Practices	Uses awareness of writing strategies, intertextuality, and text design to influence different audiences and interest groups	I guide students through the construction of a movie review, looking at how the film reviewer weaves the components of a review together.	• Individually, students produce a mini-guide to their chosen text. They explore the writing of others. • In groups, writing together, students produce a critical review of the book that they would like to win the Meyer Middle School Medal for the Best Americana Text. They are reminded that this is a persuasive text, and they should use the persuasive tips discussed in language arts class to manipulate and influence their audience.
Discussion Across Texts	Participates in social and academic talk to understand, critique, or debate various perspectives within and across a set of texts	I lead several class discussions that build into individual or small-group work. First, I discuss the components of Ebert's film review with the students and construct a list of the elements that make up a film review. I also discuss the Michael L. Printz Award criteria and help students get ready to produce their own criteria.	1. Students discuss the elements of a film review with me. 2. Students present their mini-guide to the rest of the class and place their mini-guide on the ratings scale. 3. Students work in groups to formulate three criteria for the Meyer Middle School Medal for the Best Americana Text. 4. Students work in groups to nominate a text. 5. Students work in groups to decide a final winner.
Vocabulary	Recognizes and analyzes the way that language and vocabulary influence readers, listeners, and viewers	N/A	N/A
Intertextual Connections	Recognizes and assumes that texts are not neutral, and explores the perspectives within and across texts	I explain the making-connections reading strategy before students work on journaling so that students are already thinking about intertexuality. I also ask students to complete a mini-guide to their chosen text by answering a number of questions that relate to authorial purpose and audience perspectives.	• Students individually produce a mini-guide to their chosen Americana text. Part of the guide requires them to consider audience and authorial purpose. • During the panel session, students ask critical questions to help them decide on a winning text. • To decide upon a nomination and an eventual winner, students need to consider the merits of a variety of texts.
Engagement	Actively participates in analyzing, critiquing, and questioning texts from different perspectives as readers, listeners, or viewers	I explain the power that the reader has in the text/author/reader triangle, and I provide students with independent and group opportunities to become text critics. I model active participation by sharing my own reading text and mini-guide.	• All students actively engaged at all times • Independent written work • Group discussion • Panel-session: asking questions, answering questions, or listening to answers • Group review writing
Reading Practices	Develops identities that consider different meanings and perspectives constructed and produced to elicit particular responses	I explain that readers react differently to different texts, and compare the reader to a film reviewer. A film reviewer does more than just watch and understand the film – just as a reader should do more than just read to comprehend a story.	• Journaling details the individual reader's reaction. • Mini-guide explores authorial purpose, differing perspectives, and individual reaction. • Analyze and respond to the texts of others.

Figure 5.5 This chart shows how all of the instructional dispositions are integrated into Stephanie's text-critic lessons.

© 2010 Strop and Carlson

Lesson Aims	Lesson Sequence Details
I want my students to know: • How to become a text critic – what the role entails • The components of a film review – what the film reviewer looks for • The kinds of questions they need to ask in order to take on the role of text critic • How to establish criteria to determine a good-quality text with a wide-ranging audience • How to truly evaluate a text • How to work in groups to make critical decisions	1. I introduce and explain the role of reader as film reviewer; I talk about the reader/text/author triangle and the power that the reader has. 2. I read two web film reviews by Roger Ebert with the rest of the class. 3. I identify the components of a film review. What kinds of things does Ebert write about? 4. I set mini-guide task: Students are to design a small booklet that focuses on six critical questions that will encourage them to think like a film reviewer. 5. I show students my own mini-guide on *Bone by Bone by Bone* by Tony Johnston, and discuss her responses with her students. 6. Students spend two lessons working on their mini-guide. While students work, I construct a giant ratings scale on a spare wall. 7. I ask students to prepare a minute-long presentation on their mini-guide, highlighting some of the most important comments they made. 8. Students present their mini-guides and, at the end of the presentation, place their mini-guide on the ratings scale. Placing the guide at the top signifies excellence; placing it at the bottom denotes the text made poor reading. 9. I introduce the idea of a Meyer Middle School Medal for the best Americana text. 10. Using the Michael L. Printz Award criteria as a model, students work in groups to decide on three criteria for our school medal. 11. I gather each group's criteria to create our class criteria for the medal. 12. Students return to their groups to nominate a book from yesterday's presentations that they believe should win the medal. 13. We hear nominations and reveal plans for the next class: hold a panel session where the audience gets to ask the students who read the nominated book questions. The questions should reflect their role as text critics, and the answers should help each group decide which text deserves to win. 14. Groups work on a list of questions to ask the students during the panel discussion. Students with the nominated texts can listen in to the group discussions but must not take part in them. 15. Panel question-and-answer session takes place. 16. Students return to the groups to choose a final winner and write a critical review supporting their decision. 17. Final votes are tallied.

Figure 5.6 Stephanie's text-critic lesson plans – at a glance

Text Type	Linguistic (oral/written language)	Visual (still/moving images)	Auditory (music/sound)	Gestural (facial expression/body language)	Spatial (layout/organization of objects in space)
Roger Ebert film reviews from web	Paragraphs, rating systems, and captions	Photograph from movie	N/A	N/A	The arrangement of the subjects and other objects within the photograph
Fiction novel; example: *Crackback* by John Coy	Chapter book	Jacket design	N/A	N/A	• Layout of text and chapters • Order and construction of novel
Travel book; example: *Walk Across America* by Peter Jenkins	Prose Dialogue Dialect/cultural language Quotations	Photographs Maps Jacket design	N/A	Analyze people and places via photographs	• Layout of text and chapters • Arrangement of pictures and captions
Nonfiction book; example: *Revenge of the Whale* by Nathaniel Philbrick	Prose Quotations Headings Subheadings Primary sources Original documents	Photographs Maps Pictures Paintings Timelines	N/A	Analyze people and places via photographs	Layout devices – boxes, tables, charts, headings, image placement
Poetry; example: *Out of the Dust* by Karen Hesse	Language Dialogue Imagery Word choice	• Placement of words on the page • Illustrations	N/A	N/A	• Form and layout • Organization of poetry

Adapted from: Anstey and Bull 2006

Figure 5.7 Stephanie's text selections for her text-critic lessons

Text Type	Semiotic System	Genre	Learning Purpose	What Students Need to Know	What Students Need to Be Able to Do
Film Review Students choose their texts from an assortment of texts that include:	Linguistic Visual Spatial	Web text	• Understand how to create meaning using image-based texts • Understand the role of the reader as film reviewer • Verbally discuss and present ideas about these texts to the rest of the class • Create own visual text	• How to become a text critic – what the role entails • The components of a film review – what the film reviewer looks for • The kinds of questions to ask in order to take on the role of text critic • How to establish criteria to determine a good-quality text with a wide-ranging audience • How to truly evaluate a text	• Read two film reviews, and analyze for the essential elements • Complete their own critical mini-guide to the book by answering six key questions • Rate their book using a scale of poor–excellent • Work in groups to establish the criteria of a great text with wide-ranging appeal • Work in groups to decide on a winning text with wide-ranging appeal • Work in groups to create and write a critical and influential text review
Novel	Linguistic Visual Spatial	Fiction			
Travel Book	Linguistic Visual Gestural Spatial	Nonfiction			
Nonfiction	Linguistic Visual Gestural Spatial	Nonfiction			
Poetry	Linguistic Visual Spatial				

Adapted from Anstey and Bull 2006

Figure 5.8 Stephanie's text analysis for her text-critic lessons

*   *   *

Stephanie illustrated how students became text critics through a number of different, well-planned methods. Their experiences with code breaking, meaning making, and text using supported their engagement in the analysis and interpretation of the selected texts. Beginning with definitions of Americana and transitioning to students' self-selected texts, Stephanie assisted students in their review of contemporary adolescent novels and then the evaluation of those works within the theme of Americana.

As students began to internalize the four resources, they started to use them as stepping stones to higher-level thinking and analysis of multiple texts.

Holly: Gatsby and the American Dream Unit

By this point, students have experienced breaking codes, making meaning, and using text. They have explored different social and cultural contexts while defining various characters' struggles to achieve the American Dream. In their new role as text critic, students return to *The Great Gatsby* to catalyze a *personal* view of their own American Dream. Just as a film reviewer comments on the realism and relevance of a film, students will look at the universal elements of Gatsby's quest for the American Dream and at how F. Scott Fitzgerald's portrayal determines whether or not his work is "eternally modern." In the following lesson, students draw upon perspectives from the whole MTS to create a web-based presentation that captures the evolution of their own American dreams.

Students are launched into a critical look at the timelessness and relevance of *The Great Gatsby* via an introduction to "universality" (characters and themes that transcend time and culture) as it is used in literary analysis. Students take their understanding of this term and closely examine the perspectives offered by two newspaper articles, "Eternally Modern: Fitzgerald Connects Jazz Age to Generation X" and "Teens Connect with Jay Gatsby and His Dream." Students read the two articles and individually complete some comprehension questions aimed at identifying the authors' main arguments and support for those arguments.

After reading "Eternally Modern," students are asked the following three questions:

1. What "thesis" or main argument is the writer making?
2. What examples support this argument?
3. What arguments can you make to counter the writer's view?

After reading the article "Teens Connect," students are asked the following five questions:

1. What is the writer's main point from a teacher's perspective?
2. What examples support the teacher's perspective?
3. What is the article's main point from a student's perspective?
4. What examples support the student's perspective?
5. How closely do these perspectives match your own view? Explain. (For example, one student responded: *I agree that the American Dream is dependent on both financial security and the will power to achieve goals.*)

Students then work in pairs or small groups to summarize the commonalities and different perspectives in the arguments presented. This exercise teaches students how to interpret different views and transform them into their own arguments. Essentially, teen readers are critically reading two articles that they may or may not connect to their lives. Likewise, they may see themselves as part of the collective generation that viewed Gatsby as a remote dreamer or fool, not the archetypal American Dreamer. One student offers this observation: "I feel best about the 'Teens Connect' article because I think it relates better to people, while 'Eternally Modern' is more of a generalization about Fitzgerald's life. I agree that 'the best way to [connect] diverse students is with books that mirror their lives' so they can see that other people have the same problems."

An extension of this becomes each "text critic's" response to this blog prompt: "Agree or disagree with this statement: A major reason Fitzgerald is eternally modern is due to his interpretation of the American Dream." In this exercise students can argue varying points of view; that is, whether or not Fitzgerald really is "eternally modern," and, if he is, can that be tied to his interpretation of the American Dream? If students' responses are posted to a site that offers threaded discussion, the site can offer fertile ground for continued class discussion and debate.

At this juncture, it is important to return to the graphic organizer that was introduced early in the unit (see figure 5.9). It offers a visual way for students to connect the many character and author voices that they have encountered. Students can add to this visual as an individual or group exercise. By having the discussion focus on the integrative aspects of the graphic, students are charged with bringing together multiple perspectives from all the texts in the unit – just as they did in the panel

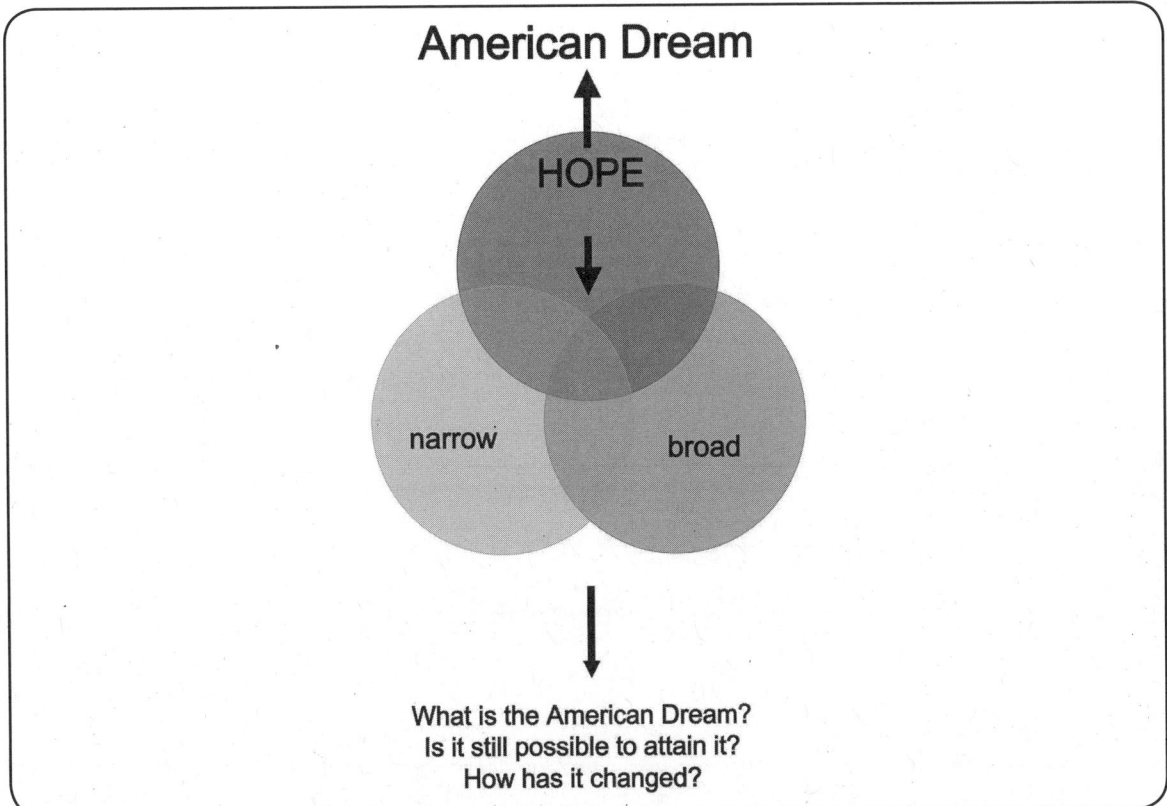

American Dream

HOPE

narrow   broad

What is the American Dream?
Is it still possible to attain it?
How has it changed?

Figure 5.9 Initial graphic organizer and essential questions for the American Dream unit

interviews (see chapter 3). Revisiting this graphic also gives students another way to connect texts and to synthesize perspectives on factors like the role of hope, social contexts, and immigrant status in the attainability of the American Dream.

At this point, I introduce the cumulative assessment for the unit: Produce a "Personal American Dream" in the form of a VoiceThread presentation. VoiceThread is an online tool that allows students to narrate, use accompanying photos and images, and obtain feedback from others through several sources.

I provide the following focus questions to help students draw intertextual connections to their personal hopes and goals:

- How would you express the hopes and goals you have for yourself as a teen, and eventually, as an adult?

- How does your American Dream remind you of the dream of other characters and voices from our MTS?

- How would others from different backgrounds, power hierarchies, or social and historical contexts react to your American Dream?

- How "universal" are the elements of your American Dream? Whose voice and views would not serve as complements to your American Dream?

- With whom (both real people and characters from MTS) would you choose to share your American Dream?

- Would your American Dream inspire anyone else or the American Dream of someone else?

- What text formats (for example, print, graphic, digital) would best portray and communicate your American Dream?

Students use the questions as guidelines for their VoiceThread presentations as they write the "narrative script," choose the images to accompany the script, and solicit feedback from peers and others. Generally, this project takes several days to plan and about two to three days of computer lab time. Then, as a culminating activity, students share their VoiceThread presentations with the whole class.

Holly's Text-Critic Lessons

Instructional Disposition	Text Critic	Teaching Examples	Examples of Students' Work
Writing Practices	Uses awareness of writing strategies, intertextuality, and text design to influence different audiences and interest groups	I have students read two newspaper articles on Fitzgerald's connection to today's teens and respond to a blog prompt.	Students respond to the blog prompt "Agree or disagree with this statement: A major reason Fitzgerald is eternally modern is due to his interpretation of the American Dream (AD)."
Discussion Across Texts	Participates in social and academic talk to understand, critique, or debate various perspectives within and across a set of texts	I review our previous discussion formats to focus on characterization, universality, and the AD to help students respond to the essential questions and formulate their own AD. This discussion is connected to a revisiting of the AD Anticipation Guide and the AD graphic organizer introduced at the beginning of the unit.	Students create personal versions of AD graphic organizers to integrate their perspectives with those they have been discussing and reading about.
Vocabulary	Recognizes and analyzes the ways that language and vocabulary influence readers, listeners, and viewers	I teach that the term *universality* can apply to any literary analysis.	Students integrate the terms used throughout the unit and build arguments around the term *universality* to critique Gatsby's AD (and, ultimately, their own).
Intertextual Connections	Recognizes and assumes that texts are not neutral, and explores the perspectives within and across texts	I guide students to consider several key questions that focus on (1) how various characters in the MTS influence our ADs, and (2) how our "MTS Tour" stimulates connections to our individual ADs.	Students individually produce web-based presentations to describe the evolution and influences on their own ADs. These culminating projects draw upon all the texts from the unit and reflect the influence of specific texts.
Engagement	Actively participates in analyzing, critiquing, and questioning texts from different perspectives as readers, viewers, or listeners	I help students organize their thinking about their own "immigrant status" and how that empowers them and shapes their AD.	Students draw on all selections in the MTS to formulate their own ADs.
Reading Practices	Develops an expectation that considers different meanings and perspectives constructed and produced to elicit particular responses	I have students set purpose by introducing the blog prompt they will respond to after they read two newspaper articles: "Eternally Modern: Fitzgerald Connects Jazz Age to Generation X" and "Teens Connect with Jay Gatsby and His Dream."	Students read the two newspaper articles and individually complete some comprehension questions. Then, they work in pairs or small groups to summarize the commonalities and different perspectives in the arguments presented in the two articles.

Figure 5.10 This chart shows how all of the instructional dispositions are integrated into Holly's text-critic lessons.

Lesson Aims	Lesson Sequence Details
I want my students to know: • How to be text critics and view MTS from different perspectives, both present and absent • How to examine universality through the lens of the American Dream (AD) • How to use a "cumulative" graphic organizer to compare elements of the AD through the lens of a different text • How to create their own visual text and narrative of their personal ADs	1. I introduce student to the two articles on Gatsby's connections to modern generations. I have students work in pairs or small groups to identify the major assertions and supporting evidence while examining their commonalities and differences. 2. Students respond to the prompt "Agree or disagree with this statement: A major reason Fitzgerald is eternally modern is due to his interpretation of the American Dream." Students could post their responses to a discussion board that offers threaded discussion. 3. Students return to the unit's graphic organizer to work individually or in small groups to bring together dominant patterns (e.g., responses to the idea of the superficiality and sustainability of the AD). Students work to synthesize perspectives on the varying dimensions of the attainability of the AD. 4. Students articulate verbally and visually their "Personal American Dreams" via VoiceThread presentations that encourage reflection on all the ADs they have encountered in the MTS.

Figure 5.11 Holly's text-critic lesson plans – at a glance

Text Type	Linguistic (oral/written language)	Visual (still/moving images)	Auditory (music/ sound)	Gestural (facial expresion/ body language)	Spatial (layout/organization of objects in space)
Newspaper article	Captions, headings, paragraphs	Photographs of Fitzgerald	N/A	N/A	Arrangement of print and subject of photographs
Blog entry	Original entries vs. threaded discussion entries	N/A	N/A	N/A	N/A

Adapted from Anstey and Bull 2006

Figure 5.12 Holly's text selections for her text-critics lessons

Text Type	Semiotic System	Genre	Learning Purpose	What Students Need to Know	What Students Need to Be Able to Do
Newspaper article	Linguistic Visual Spatial	Nonfiction	To understand the term *universality* as it applies to two articles arguing that Gatsby's quest is universal	• What text critics do • How modern journalists describe Fitzgerald's impact on today's teens	Connect the viewpoints of two journalists to their own view of Gatsby's universality
Blog entry	Linguistic Visual Spatial	Personal writing	To discuss in writing their interpretations of arguments focused on Fitzgerald and his Gatsby character	• How universality and being labeled "eternally modern" can be complementary • How the concept of the AD unites Gatsby to the other characters in the MTS	Defend in writing a view of Fitzgerald as "eternally modern" as he interprets the AD

Adapted from Anstey and Bull 2006

Figure 5.13 Holly's text analysis for her text-critic lessons

*   *   *

In this lesson, Holly used technology to empower students to comment on and voice their perspective about the theme of the unit. VoiceThreads and blogging introduced new ways for students to engage in discourse about the American Dream – ways of communication that adolescents are proficient in and enjoy doing. The students rose to the challenge and demonstrated deeper knowledge of the theme, *The Great Gatsby*, Fitzgerald, and additional supporting texts. Holly assisted students in thinking like film reviewers. Thus, the students became analyzers, synthesizers, position-takers (Bourdieu 1998), and articulators of opinion and understanding.

Richard: Vietnam War Unit

As practiced code breakers, skilled meaning makers, and savvy text users, my students put all of their skills as literate thinkers into play and, as a summary assessment, create a multimedia text set of their own called "Truth Poems for Two (or More!) Voices." The framework for this invention is a variation on Paul Fleischman's *Joyful Noise: Poems for Two Voices*. Poetry for two or more voices is a multi-column format that allows writers to juxtapose contrasting ideas, concepts, or perspectives inside the frame of a single work. This technique requires synthesizing multiple perspectives into a single, coherent "media text."

Students create poems using their own words and words from other media sources they select (books, stories, newspapers, websites, film, music, news reports, or broadcasts). The poems focus on a current, recent, or historical issue (such as the Vietnam War or the war in Iraq) and its attendant social, economic, political, and emotional impacts. In self-selected small groups, students develop an arguable position on an issue, then collect and research various texts that help them develop their ideas.

Advanced work will synthesize a minimum of six different sources/texts to create the "poem" and to support and advance the "argument." All presentations must include the following:

- At least one Internet-sourced print text that a group member has discovered
- At least one non-Internet-sourced book or magazine print text that a group member has discovered
- At least one audio text (a song, sound effect, or other recording)
- At least one original text written by group member(s)
- At least one appropriate (large scale/for classroom viewing) visual text

The work is formatted into separate columns – one column for each "voice" or group member. Alternating lines indicate alternating viewpoints, and each line is read by its author. Adjacent lines represent agreement or compromise and are, therefore, read in unison.

To begin, we go back and review the statements from the anticipation guide (see page xxx); I press for shifts in opinions or look for reinforced views. This time, students have more thorough and cogent reasons for their assertions.

Once more, we turn back to our three essential questions:

1. How do media affect our interpretation of a news story?
2. How do multiple perspectives (e.g., different media) shape our perception of the truth?
3. What constitutes a war crime?

Students now understand the shifts in meanings based on distinctive media texts. They still struggle with the ambiguities of meaning that can accompany multiple perspectives, although most find they have a clearer picture of the "inner truth" of the events studied. Finally, most students can readily describe what constitutes a war crime, and they are more certain in their descriptions of it than they were at the beginning of the unit.

The students self-select working groups of threes and fours. Then, following the assignment outline, they research topics, collect media stories and texts, develop a position or arguable stance, and, finally, write their poems or scripts by synthesizing their resources. They are able to create their own meanings and to assert their own points of view.

Below is a section of one student group's poems. Their "poems," as did the texts we used for our code breaking and meaning making, should engage, even provoke their audience. Students must consider the "point" or "argument" they wish to make and use language and texts to support their intentions.

Finally, they present their work orally to the rest of the class, who serve as audience for these newly constructed messages.

Soldier	Lieutenant	Reporter	American Citizen
(walking)	(walking)	(enters)	(enters)
		Excuse me. Do you have a few minutes? I would like to ask a few questions about Thanh Phong and My Lai.	
Sure!	Sure!		
		What are your opinions of those evenings	
ORDERS	ORDERS	MURDER!	MURDER!
We eliminated the enemy.	We eliminated the enemy.	Innocent people were killed.	Innocent people were killed.
		Under the 1949 Geneva Conventions, collective punishments are war crimes, collective penalties, and likewise all measures of intimidation or of terrorism are prohibited. How did you justify these killings?	
	You could be court-marshaled for refusing an order in the face of an enemy.		
All orders were to be assumed legal; the soldiers' job was to carry out any order given to him to the best of his ability.			
			Be reminded that when you are ordered to engage in crimes against humanity, you must choose humanity. There is no honor in killing others like yourself for the gods of profit.
		What were the rules of engagement you and your men were following?	
	We were basically writing the rules as we went.		
			According to the Military Assistance Command, you are expected to treat women with politeness and respect, but I heard that at least one girl was raped and then killed.
		As the "search and destroy" mission unfolded, it soon degenerated into the massacre of over 300 apparently unarmed civilians including women, children, and the elderly. How did it lead to this?	
It got pretty ridiculous once the guns got going. I was in survival mode. Then something sunk into me that these people were marched into that ditch and murdered. That was the only explanation I could come up with. *(Starts moving toward reporter and citizen.)*			
(Confused look, doesn't say anything. May shrug shoulders.)	ORDERS!	MURDER!	MURDER!

Figure 5.14 Mike's group used a number of voices to produce higher-level thinking and multiple perspectives, in addition to analyzing and critiquing a number of different texts.

Richard's Text-Critic Lessons

Instructional Disposition	Text Critic	Teaching Examples	Examples of Students' Work
Writing Practices	Uses awareness of writing strategies, intertextuality, and text design to influence different audiences and interest groups	I share models of previous student work to inspire and create benchmarks for student achievement.	Students write at least a portion of their final poems or scripts for presentation to the rest of the class.
Discussion Across Texts	Participates in social and academic talk to understand, critique, or debate various perspectives within and across a set of texts	I help facilitate a final class discussion on the revisited anticipation guide and the essential questions of the unit.	Students, working in their groups with their mates, develop their own discussions centering on the idea and argument their poem will make, the texts they will use, how they will produce their own, and who is their intended audience.
Vocabulary	Recognizes and analyzes the ways that language and vocabulary influence readers, listeners, and viewers	I remind and encourage students to own the vocabulary we have collected and studied by using it in their presentations.	Students integrate the terms used throughout the unit in their final work.
Intertextual Connections	Recognizes and assumes that texts are not neutral, and explores the perspectives within and across texts	I clearly articulate some minimum requirements for the number and types of texts to be used in the final projects.	Students individually produce MTS presentations to reveal their own position relative to the idea they have chosen to research and present.
Engagement	Actively participates in analyzing, critiquing, and questioning texts from different perspectives as readers, viewers, or listeners	I help students develop a workable thesis for their "poems" and offer suggestions for finding and developing various sources for material.	Students develop rich, layered MTS that they own and care about.
Reading Practices	Develops an expectation that considers different meanings and perspectives constructed and produced to elicit particular responses	I require students to review a wide variety of possible texts.	Students find more material than they can effectively use, and must thoughtfully sift and winnow through it to create cogent, unified poems.

Figure 5.15 This chart shows how all of the instructional dispositions are integrated into Richard's text-critic lessons.

Lesson Aims	Lesson Sequence Details
I want my students to: • Activate prior knowledge and lessons • Understand the role of the reader as text critic, using the analogy of a film reviewer • Combine all of their previous reader dispositions as code breakers, meaning makers, and text users with the instructional dispositions of the text critic to create original texts synthesized from the ideas and content of the unit's MTS and their own further reading and research	1. I remind students of two essential questions of the unit: (1) How do the media affect our interpretation of a news story? (2) How do multiple perspectives shape our perception of the truth? 2. I present the role of the "text critic." Note that a text critic reacts critically to the knowledge gained from code-breaking, meaning-making, and text-using practices, then forms his or her own conclusion – or argument. Note that our work with the instructional dispositions of this role will lead to a summative assessment. Students will work together in small, self-selected groups to find and fit together various texts – in effect, to create their own MTS. They will synthesize the ideas from their texts to develop their own critical thinking and response to the ideas presented in their chosen texts. 3. I introduce the idea of "poems" for two or more voices based on Paul Fleischman's examples. Using models, I share with students examples of multi-column texts that allow for the juxtaposition of various ideas and perspectives – drawn from both found and original texts – and that develop a critical position on a "big idea" or thesis. 4. After fielding their many questions (and working to calm their fears about "writing poetry"), I ask students to brainstorm topics of significant current or historical interest. We work through a process to arrive at a workable number of topics. 5. I ask students to fit themselves into groups of 2–4, to develop an arguable position or thesis on their selected topic, and then to begin collecting and researching various texts to provoke their thinking and to help them establish their arguments. 6. I share with them with the requirements of this assessment: broadly, to create their own MTS, using at minimum six different source texts (with at least one an original text written or created by group members); to synthesize these texts into a coherent critical argument in the multi-column format of the poems for multiple voices; to present these poems to their classmates. 7. I share with them the assessment rubrics I will use to evaluate their final written and oral work, answer any remaining questions, and provide them the necessary time in class and in resource areas to complete this task.

Figure 5.16 Richard's text critic lesson plans – at a glance

Linguistic (oral/written language)	Visual (still/moving images)	Auditory (music/sound)	Gestural (facial expression/body language)	Spatial (layout/organization of objects in space)

Text selection for this part of the unit will vary by student groups according to the needs and dictates of their ideas as they relate to the purposes and argument of their "poems."

Students must employ at least six specific types of texts (representing various semiotic systems). These include:

1. *at least one* Internet-sourced print text that a group member has discovered
2. *at least one* non-Internet-sourced book or magazine print text that a group member has discovered
3. *at least one* audio text (a song, sound effect, or other recording)
4. *at least one* original text written by group member(s)
5. *at least one* appropriate (large scale/for classroom viewing) visual text (photograph, drawing, map, graph, etc.)

Adapted from Anstey and Bull 2006

Figure 5.17 Richard's text selections for his text-critic lessons

Text Type	Semiotic System	Genre	Learning Purpose	What Students Need to Know	What Students Need to Be Able to Do
Internet-sourced print text	Linguistic Visual	Prose	• Engage their own knowledge, skill sets, and patterns of practice as readers of text • Recognize familiar and obvious patterns, codes, meanings • Identify or synthesize new or different ideas, patterns, or meanings in the text	• Specific vocabulary • How to combine the resources and knowledge gained from the roles of code breaker, meaning maker, text user • How to examine disparate texts to form inferences, to speculate, to create meaning • How to use own personal experiences and background knowledge to interpret and synthesize new meanings from texts • How to take an arguable position on an issue and present it critically	• Work with partners in small groups • Develop their own MTS • Derive meaning from texts • Synthesize various textual ideas • Create their own meaning by taking a critical stance on an issue • Present work through a variety of semiotic systems
Non-Internet-sourced book or magazine print text	Linguistic Visual	Prose			
Audio text	Auditory	Music, sound effects, etc.			
Student-created text	Linguistic Visual Gestural Spatial	Will vary: prose, poetry, photographs, etc.			
Visual text	Linguistic Visual Gestural Spatial	Photograph, drawing, video, film, TV, other graphic imagery			
Poetry/Song lyrics	Visual Auditory	Poetry			

Adapted from Anstey and Bull 2006

Figure 5.18 Richard's text analysis for his text-critic lessons

* * *

This lesson demonstrated how students critically analyzed a number of different genres. Richard guided them to examine the construction, point of view, and purpose of each genre, and then he assisted them in synthesizing the information. Working together, the students integrated the information from multiple texts to develop a new text form that represented their understandings of a particular event in Vietnam. The experience empowered the students to write "poems" in which they voiced and enacted their own ideas, experiences, and purposes.

PLANNING FOR THE TEXT-CRITIC ROLE

In this chapter, lessons illustrated how students are empowered to read, analyze, and evaluate a selected text. In Stephanie's class, the students selected a text that interested them and evaluated it based on a rating scale. In Holly's class, students used technology to report their perspectives and opinions regarding the American Dream and then began to articulate their own dreams. Richard asked his students to analyze multiple texts throughout the Vietnam unit and then to articulate their understanding, critique and debate various perspectives, and, finally, to write poems for many voices (Fleischman 1989).

The three questions we asked you to consider at the beginning of this chapter are listed again. Examine and apply the questions to your own planning of a text critic lesson within MTS. After you have drafted your text-critic lesson, use the planning chart (see BLM 2, appendix B) to analyze it.

1. How are my students thinking like film reviewers and text critics?
2. How do I plan to support and encourage students to maintain and effectively use this role in their learning and monitoring?
3. Where will I integrate this role in my own practice?

Chapter 6
Reflections

In this book, we have discussed multimedia text sets (MTS) in the context of a middle-school and two high-school classrooms. The three teachers – Stephanie, Holly, and Richard – successfully used MTS that scaffolded their students' thinking and engaged them in higher-level thinking and independent learning.

Before you begin your own MTS unit, here are some bits of advice from us and some reflective thoughts on the MTS Framework (see figure 6.1) from Stephanie, Holly, and Richard.

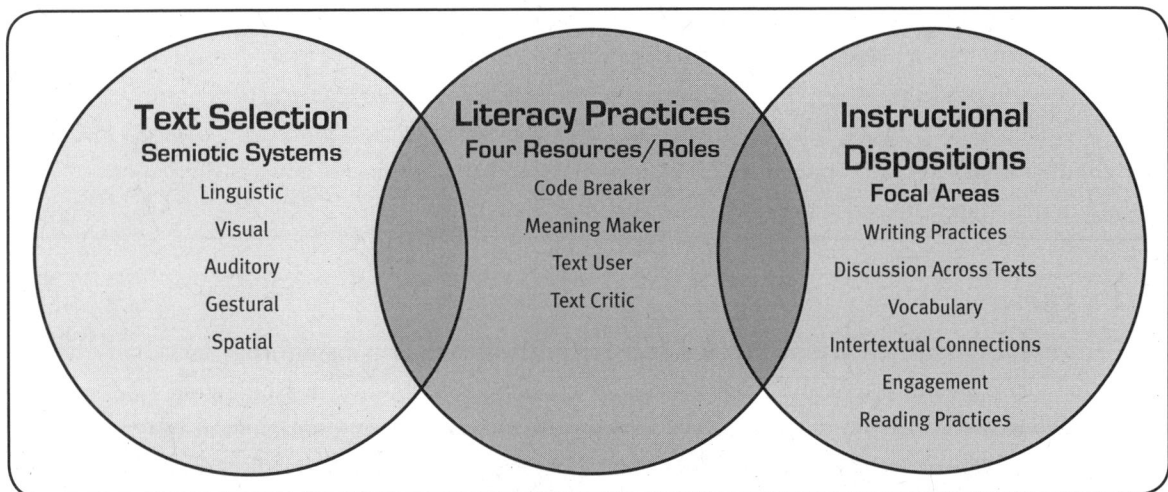

Text Selection
Semiotic Systems

Linguistic

Visual

Auditory

Gestural

Spatial

Literacy Practices
Four Resources/Roles

Code Breaker

Meaning Maker

Text User

Text Critic

Instructional Dispositions
Focal Areas

Writing Practices

Discussion Across Texts

Vocabulary

Intertextual Connections

Engagement

Reading Practices

Figure 6.1 MTS Framework

FOUR RESOURCES MODEL

The Four Resources Model is a range of literacy practices in which students engage actively in using four necessary "roles" (defined by metaphors). Using metaphors helps, because they give students access to academic talk in familiar ways and contexts – students know the "job" that each role entails.

As we reflect on the use of the roles in the Four Resources Model (Luke and Freebody 1999), we are reminded that these roles are dynamic; that is, they are continuously combined and articulated in relation to each other. Thus, the roles – code breaker, meaning maker, text user, and text critic – are not intended to be a developmental hierarchy (Luke 2000). For the purpose of understanding, we have presented these roles separately, even though it is difficult to talk about them in isolation. In practice, simultaneously relating and combining the four roles invites authentic discussions and coherent intertextual connections within and across texts.

Stephanie

The Four Resources Model has provided an excellent foundation for my lesson and curriculum planning. My approach to teaching reading has altered, because my focus has shifted. The Four Resources Model focuses on both the student and the four roles of code breaker, meaning maker, text user, and text critic rather than on a text-focused curriculum (where using strategies to unlock a text takes center stage). Students need to realize that they, not the text, are in control of any text situation. The power lies in their hands – not in the text.

In addition, I have made a definitive move away from the traditional prose-based (especially the novel) reading classroom to an innovative reading classroom that acknowledges and embraces a wide range of text types. To become truly powerful readers, our students need to be able to analyze and comprehend a wide variety of texts. They need to have as much literacy experience as possible.

I have become bolder when it comes to choosing texts for the classroom, and I am unafraid to experiment and introduce my students to new text types. This has been an exciting process. The Four Resources Model provides me with clear definitions of the different roles a reader must undertake in order to truly master a text or text genre. For me, this model has a depth that was missing from a strategy-based reading curriculum. As students move through and experience each role, they are ultimately journeying toward the role of text critic. Students need to know that they can be critical of any text they come across; they just needed to understand what that role entails.

Holly

I have expanded my definition of reading to include visual texts in many forms. As students assume the various roles, there are many more options for increasing rigor. Likewise, the diversity of texts in MTS allows me to incorporate more sociological and historical perspectives in building background knowledge and stimulating discussion about points of connection. As before, theme and essential questions about the universality of an author's view and purpose are central to instruction. Now, however, I see more pathways to helping students read "against" texts in addition to "across" texts. Finally, I now push past authorial intent and character analysis – and ask students to consider themselves and their individual schema as "text" that connects to the MTS. MTS give students who have expertise with different texts a chance to participate in high levels of thought, because familiarity with a type of text supports their ability to be text critics. They are, thus, challenged to examine the interconnectedness and universality of the MTS and its social messages in their own worlds.

I am struck with the interconnectedness of the roles and the fact that I need not always start my units with code breaking. Here is a simple example of this in the Gatsby/American Dream unit: Students who have more experience and background knowledge about the Roaring 20s or in film analysis are ready to move forward faster. Likewise, some have read more of Fitzgerald and gravitate to "authorial intent" quickly. Awareness of this offers us, as teachers, the opportunity of "instant differentiation": many students will find ways of "meaning making" by moving to deep character analysis and then returning to how the characters were shaped by their era and portrayed from various viewpoints. Meaning making is recursive, as when students build their body biographies with eyes toward the ultimate panel interview. A meaning maker establishes a base to look forward from and to look back at, continually verifying and reformulating his or her hypotheses on the characters' motives, ethics, ambitions, etc.

When students move between the roles of the Four Resources Model, they rely on the skills of text users at any stage where they need to make connections and to draw upon prior experience and background knowledge to do so. The social networkers we know as our students are reinventors by nature; they may set out to be text users instantly, but they then must rely on the foundations of code breaking and meaning making to reach their goals. Further, as our students progress through their school lives, they continuously make plans for their post-school lives – so they may have already "broken the code" on many specific aspects of their American Dreams. They naturally compare themselves to others and take inspiration from others. When they are doing this, they are reaching back into their literate and personal lives to construct different perspectives. As such, they are critics, but cannot weave a full view unless they continue to "reflect backwards." They achieve the full view through continual stops and starts, revisiting and making intertextual connections across the texts through the roles of code breaker, meaning maker, and text user. Much like the process of building a bridge that affords complete access to the "other side," our students must continually retrace their steps in order to weave together all the strands of the panoramic destinations that await them.

Richard

I have become clearer about what I am teaching and why I am teaching it. I have learned to develop clear essential questions at the start of a unit and lesson, and then to present challenging materials to students so that they can synthesize them into clear and engaging responses to these questions.

I have also become more skilled and fluid at differentiating my instruction with heterogeneous groups of students, in large part because I believe that I am better prepared as an instructor, and I employ richer and more varied content and materials.

As my fluency with this model grows, so does my fluidity with my text selection process and my lesson planning and classroom instruction. I am more focused on the learning outcomes I desire for my students, and I am clearer on how to help them improve their skills and competencies in textual literacies. The Four Resources Model provides a solid framework for my thinking as I develop various text sets and the essential questions at the heart of our lessons.

INSTRUCTIONAL DISPOSITIONS

In chapter 1, we presented the instructional dispositions chart, which listed the essential elements of the literacy practices in the Four Resources Model and the six instructional dispositions. We have recreated the original chart again here for easy reference as you begin to plan your MTS (see figure 6.2). Refer to this chart when considering what instructional dispositions you plan to integrate into your lesson. Holly advises beginning with the role of code breaker to test drive your MTS before you ratchet up the conceptual hierarchies to meaning maker, text user, and text critic. When you are ready, continue building on each of the four roles, and use this chart to focus your thinking.

Stephanie

I feel that the instructional dispositions chart represents an important analysis of the act of reading. The horizontal columns of code breaker, meaning maker, text user, and text critic allow students to understand the complex job of the reader, and students also learn that they can move into each role depending on the text that they are reading. We are all struggling readers at some point, so the role of code breaker comes into play on those occasions. Comprehension and meaning making are essential parts of the act of reading. I think the most neglected roles, and yet the most significant roles, are those of text user and text critic.

I do not think enough students realize that the intent of an author has a huge impact on the texts that authors create. Students do not see through the words to the person shaping the words and (possibly) manipulating the audience. It is important that students pay attention to authorial purpose and analyze it, because this is how readers can become powerful. No author can manipulate or persuade a reader who is aware of the text-user role. Similarly powerful is the text-critic role. From this outlook, students can survey the textual landscape and evaluate it on several different levels and from a variety of perspectives. No text can shy away from the text critic. Students are so easily intimidated by complex texts; an understanding of this role, building upon an understanding of the other roles, prevents this intimidation.

The vertical column (instructional dispositions), however, is also important. In my classroom, students have expressed surprise at the fact that I require them to write, discuss, and engage with a text (as opposed to read it to just be done). Teachers have expressed surprise that I allow students more than two weeks to interact with the same book. For me, reading is all about thinking – and the reader is thinking when he or she writes about the text, discusses the book with others, forms intertextual connections, and engages with the books. It is critical that all teachers of reading incorporate each of these elements within their reading classrooms and that students have the chance to develop breadth of interaction and not just depth.

Reading strategies, as many researchers have pointed out, are valuable, but the teaching of reading does not begin and end with teaching reading strategies. Reading strategies are a piece of the reading puzzle – not the whole thing.

Instructional Disposition	Code Breaker	Meaning Maker	Text User	Text Critic
Writing Practices	Uses text conventions to write and communicate in different genres and text forms for different purposes	Uses understandings to compose and design meaningful texts for various audiences and purposes	Uses knowledge to understand and shape writing by selecting different alternatives to fit social and academic situations	Uses awareness of writing strategies, intertextuality, and text design to influence different audiences and interest groups
Discussion Across Texts	Participates in social and academic talk to communicate and express thinking about different text forms, patterns, and conventions	Participates in social and academic talk that deliberately integrates prior knowledge with new knowledge to make connections across text types and generate new, communal meanings	Participates in social and academic talk to differentiate and identify the purposes, uses, and contexts of different text forms	Participates in social and academic talk to understand, critique, or debate various perspectives within and across a set of texts
Vocabulary	Recognizes and uses vocabulary within contexts, content areas, or situations	Recognizes variations in language across contexts to understand and compose meaning in a wide range of genres and content areas	Recognizes and uses vocabulary for different purposes and contexts	Recognizes and analyzes the ways that language and vocabulary influence readers, listeners, and viewers
Intertextual Connections	Recognizes and synthesizes patterns and conventions across texts and the different meanings within different forms and contexts	Recognizes and compares the structures, responses, and possible readings across texts in different contexts	Recognizes the construction and shapes of different meanings within and across text forms	Recognizes and assumes that texts are not neutral, and explores the perspectives within and across texts
Engagement	Actively participates in decoding and encoding both familiar and new text forms	Actively participates in reading and writing to make meaning and think about a range of meanings across text forms	Actively participates in using background knowledge to inquire about and use different text forms	Actively participates in analyzing, critiquing, and questioning texts from different perspectives as readers, viewers, or listeners
Reading Practices	Develops identities that incorporate routines that value competence in breaking the code across all text types	Develops identities that include the use of meaning-making tools and prior knowledge to understand content in different contexts	Develops identities that use, analyze, and compare the way texts are shaped by intent and contexts	Develops identities that consider different meanings and perspectives constructed and produced to elicit particular responses

Figure 6.2 The intersection of literacy practices and instructional dispositions

In my school district, language arts and reading are separated. I think that the dispositions chart is an important reminder of the unbreakable relationship between reading and writing: the two are inextricably entwined. You cannot be a great writer if you cannot appreciate great writing. Every text students read and engage with acts as a model for students' own writing. It always amazes me how influential the texts we use in my writing classes are.

Holly

When choosing which of the instructional dispositions best fits the academic goal at various stages of the lesson, I consider how successful units are built; that is, in what "stage" of the lesson or unit we are focused: frontloading, guiding comprehension, or consolidating learning.

For the most part, the *vocabulary* frontloading provides background and builds understanding before students begin to discuss or apply reading practices. *Engagement* takes students from introductory or foundational material to a point where they have the "ammunition" to decode and encode any new texts. I model and encourage a variety of *reading practices* to guide comprehension and scaffold to build independent application of strategies. This allows students to build confidence and gives them a platform from which to consolidate their learning, most typically in *writing*.

Finally, promoting *discussion across texts*, both in class and via computer, is almost always the best way to assess the skills tied to making meaningful *intertextual connections*. Even struggling students respond well to the modeling of their peers as they use discussion to identify patterns and pinpoint conventions across text. This is almost always the end goal of my instruction.

Further, drawing on the instructional dispositions in such a sequence allows students to continually practice skills that enable them to connect greater numbers of text in increasingly sophisticated ways. Thus, students employ more semiotic systems and grow in their ability to navigate beyond the role of code breaker or meaning maker to become text users and text critics.

Richard

My own needs as a learner, and those of my students from past practice, help me to frame the sequencing and presentations of the instructional dispositions. Like them, when confronted with new information or new challenges, I seek out context for the new information and work to define new ideas and learn new vocabulary. This work is seminal, and I cannot imagine starting in any other place.

Framing an initial lesson by establishing the context and building vocabulary allows for successful code breaking. Once these skills have been put into play and practiced, we can become meaning makers, referencing single texts and then making connections between similar – even different – texts in the assembled text sets. It is the practiced repetition and pattern of this code breaking and meaning making that leads to students becoming successful text users and text critics. The authentic self-confidence students acquire propels them into the subtleties and nuances required of text users and text critics. Then they are on their way to becoming mature, sophisticated readers, thinkers, and writers.

TEXT SELECTION

In MTS, as in all instruction, the text selection is critical to the success of student engagement and learning. The texts need to capture attention, connect intensely to the content, and be relevant to the audience. We believe students need a variety of texts to engage in different perspectives and different ideas. Variety also gives students opportunities to learn to articulate their own thinking and connections through discussion and writing. We need to expand the literacy experience or "literacy repertoire" of our students (Luke and Freebody 1999) and think about the semiotic systems that make up different compositions of texts (Kress 2003).

Selecting texts for an effective and balanced MTS can be a challenge. With various media resources such as television, film, online resources, and music, winnowing what will engage students and aid in focusing their attention while maintaining the integrity of the content can be daunting. We believe guiding questions and visual organizers can aid in making these decisions more readily.

Historically, oral and written language has dominated the classroom curriculum. There has been a shift in this traditional way of teaching as the texts in adolescents' hands are increasingly multimodal. We need to use this as an advantage and teach to students' prior knowledge and interests. By documenting the texts we are using visually, as with the text selection planning guide, we can begin to create a unit that balances literacy practices and teaches to students' strengths. Be aware that although building a strong selection of texts will take time and revision, it is also an evolving process that engages both teachers and students.

Stephanie

I do not think I ever stop selecting texts for my MTS units. I constantly have my eyes and ears open. I find myself printing articles from online newspapers, saving clippings from magazine subscriptions, archiving YouTube clips, investigating the new books shelf in my school's media center, and making playlists of songs that fit the thematic units I teach. A portion of my yearly budget goes toward "books." I buy as many books and resources as my budget allows. The texts I focus on are the texts I find the most interesting and am passionately excited to show off in the classroom – not the texts that I know the most about (see figure 6.3). I like the exploration aspect as much as my students do. My text selections are also made with my students very much in mind. I also look to include a wide variety of text types – both traditional and non-traditional.

Text Type	Linguistic (oral/written language)	Visual (still/moving images)	Auditory (music/sound)	Gestural (facial expression/body language)	Spatial (layout/organization of objects in space)
Hampton Sides quote	Prose, paragraphs on pages	Imagery used within text	N/A	N/A	N/A
Young adult fiction	Prose, dialogue, text/email, language	Imagery, Cover, book design	N/A	Analyze descriptions of characters – show not tell, book cover	Layout of text – form, chapter arrangement
Travel books	Prose, dialogue, dialect and cultural language, quotations	Photographs, maps, book cover	N/A	Photographs: body language	Layout of text – space and arrangement of pictures and print
Nonfiction books	Prose, quotations, headings and subheadings	Photographs, maps, pictures, paintings, timeline	N/A	Analyze people and places – body language, expressions	Layout devices – boxes, tables, charts, symbols, headings, image placement
Graphic novels and cartoons	Dialogue, captions	Interactions of frames	N/A	Expressions and portrayal of characters and places – use of color and ink	Layout and size of frames, patterns in design
Picture books	Prose, dialogue, poetry, song lyrics	Illustrations and artwork	CD: music and vocal interpretation	Gesture, expression, body language	Text and image layout and design
This American Life: Radio	Dialogue, stories told, song lyrics	Use of description	Voice: tone, emphasis Music Sound effects	N/A	Arrangement and ordering of segments
Music across the decades	Song lyrics: cultural context and message	N/A	Voice: tone, emphasis, musical style, instruments used	N/A	Arrangement of verse and chorus Repetition
Poetry	Language, dialogue, imagery, word choice	Placement of words, Illustrations	N/A	N/A	Form and layout

Adapted from Anstey and Bull 2006

Figure 6.3 Stephanie used this text selection chart for her unit about Americana.

Holly

Start small; think big! I started with *The Great Gatsby*, a book I had taught many times. As a cultural artifact, this novel was the wellspring. From there, I pulled in Gatsby commentaries and remakes, as well as visuals that characterized the Jazz Age. The abundance of quality young-adult literature about the "new" immigrants made the text set easy to construct and expand (see figure 6.4).

Start with a small number of guiding questions so that you and your students are not overwhelmed. Begin with a cornerstone or seminal text that you love. Grab ideas from as many print and visual texts as you can, always with an eye on accessibility for varying levels of learners. Visit the video stores and bookstores, and ask your students for their suggestions. Look for connections that may be less literary and more historical or sociological.

Text Type	Linguistic (oral/written language)	Visual (still/moving images)	Auditory (music/sound)	Gestural (facial expression/body language)	Spatial (layout/organization of objects in space)
Classic novel	Prose, dialogue, vocabulary, style	Book Cover	N/A	N/A	N/A
Classic film	Dialogue, tone, volume, pitch, rate, regionalisms, slang of the era	DVD cover	Sound effects, music	Actors' expressions and movements	Actors' distance from each other ("social bubbles")
Roaring 20s still images	Captions	Photographs of historic, social, and political events of the era	N/A	Expressions and body language of those in photographs	Camera shots and focus; background
Young adult novels	Prose, dialogue, vocabulary, style	Book cover	N/A	N/A	N/A
Modern films	Dialogue, tone, volume, pitch, rate, dialect	DVD cover	Sound effects, music	Actors' expressions and movements	Actors' distance from each other ("social bubbles")
Newspaper article	Captions, headings, paragraphs	Photographs of Fitzgerald	N/A	N/A	Arrangement of print and subject of photographs
Blog entry	Original entries vs. threaded discussion entries	N/A	N/A	N/A	N/A

Adapted from Anstey and Bull 2006

Figure 6.4 Holly used this text selection chart for her unit about the American Dream.

Richard

This has evolved from an early (small) set of texts – rather serendipitously found and collected – to more sophisticated, deliberate, and nuanced collections of texts (see figure 6.5). Over time, collaboration with fellow teachers, my own reading and research, and students themselves have all contributed to the selection process. I aim to find texts that entertain as well as provoke, that enlighten as well as cause wonder, and that combine accessibility with challenge. It is an organic process that is constantly evolving.

Text Type	Linguistic (oral/written language)	Visual (still/moving images)	Auditory (music/sound)	Gestural (facial expression/body language)	Spatial (layout/organization of objects in space)
Political cartoon	Dialogue	Images of Thanh Phong, stripes like American flag	N/A	Expressions and body language of the reporter, bird-man, dead bodies	Cartoon space foregrounds images of dead bodies, bird-man behind stripes and haze
NY Times article	Report of incident and recent interviews	Image of Bob Kerrey on the cover	N/A	Serious expression	Half of Kerrey's face is shaded in a close-up of his face
60 Minutes video	Interview transcripts	Interviews, video footage	Voices of interviews, music, sound of helicopter	Expressions of interviewer and Kerrey, Klann, and Vietnamese woman	Camera shots of Kerrey and Klann portray them differently
Rules of Engagement	Pocket card of rules	Designed to carry in pocket	N/A	N/A	Bold print, short phrases
National Archives Photograph	N/A	Photographs of Vietnam, soldiers, and Vietnamese people	N/A	Expressions and body language of people	Camera shots and focus
Short fiction stories	Narrative and dialogue	Illustrations	N/A	N/A	Placement of illustrations
Post-traumatic stress articles	Information	Diagrams	N/A	N/A	Placement of diagrams
Vietnam movies	Dialoguesubtitles	Narrative and archived footage,editing	Music, sound, dialogue	Body language, expressions, and movement	Camera shots and angles
Songs about Vietnam	Lyrics	Music videoEditing	Music, singing, acoustics	Body language, expressions, and movement	Camera shots and angles

Adapted from Anstey and Bull 2006

Figure 6.5 Richard used this text selection chart for his unit about the Vietnam War.

STUDENTS' RESPONSE

Stephanie, Holly, and Richard have had solid success with building their MTS and using the MTS framework in their teachings. The MTS framework has provided a foundation for thinking, essential questions, text selection, and planning. These three teachers are not the only ones who grew in the experience when changing their approach. The approach has had a profound effect on their students.

Stephanie

After being initially concerned at the lack of novels we were covering in my reading/language arts curriculum, my students learned to feel comfortable exploring, creating, and critiquing a range of text types. They realized that reading requires the reader to actively inhabit a number of roles, and that a different kind of thinking is required for fulfillment of each role. They also realized that reading is not a black-and-white process: reading is about exploring – digging around in text. It is not about right or wrong, true or false. The reader calls the shots – not the teacher and not the book. My students learn that every text type and every text can be explored and interpreted and that they are in charge of such investigations.

Holly

Relieved that they would not be expected to write a traditional literary analysis paper, my students were still suspicious that I was "teaching the class like a college seminar!" They appreciated the choices of texts they were offered and the diversity of the MTS. In addition, they were happy to have many options to create visual renditions to reflect understanding and mastery. Last, they welcomed the challenge of connecting their own American Dreams to both "old and new" immigrants.

Richard

In general, my students have responded vigorously to the variety and breadth of materials and texts presented in the text sets. All of them have found something of value in the text sets presented. In the early stages of this work, some struggled with synthesizing the material, especially in response/relationship to the essential questions. In time, based on my revision of the questions and their own practiced ability to read across texts, their skills in each category of the Four Resources Model grew. This naturally fostered an increased confidence and willingness to engage with the texts, the ideas they presented, and with one another.

FINAL THOUGHTS

Multimedia Text Sets will help you begin to expand your teaching to include a variety of text materials, incorporate higher-level thinking by teaching adolescents how to read, deconstruct, and make intertextual connections. This book will help you with instructional planning that will increase comprehension, writing, discussion, vocabulary, engagement, and increase opportunities to participate in a variety of literacy practices. This book will help you reach beyond printed and oral text, expand perspectives, and transcend strategy-based instruction. It will take time and planning, and it will take analysis and deeper thinking.

We encourage you to take those first steps. Become bolder when it comes to choosing texts and approaching them in varied ways. Be constantly on the lookout for different text types that fit your teaching theme and purpose. Post your essential questions on the wall, and refer to them each time you clip an article, listen to the lyrics of a generational song, or each time a student brings you a new piece of text to share. Continue to self question, reflect, and revise. Remember the adolescent learners: What is important to them? What do they want to talk about, write about, and question? Holly advises, "Provide opportunities for student choice. Remember that learners naturally respond to "connectedness." That connectedness will capture thinking and scaffold learning to achieve comprehension.

Richard recommends, "Be fearless! Be willing to make that leap out of your own comfort zone, and to replace the familiar and routine with the new (or unknown) and the out of the ordinary."

Finally, remember that well planned MTS can change your teaching life. Stephanie states, "The model has given me a language and an easily understandable series of comparisons that enables me to articulate easily and clearly the four literacy roles to my students. New life has been breathed into my lesson planning and curriculum building, and I wouldn't have it any other way."

As the teachers' work and words have illustrated, using the MTS framework has helped them make the shift from linguistics to semiotics. In the process, it has changed their teaching and their students' thinking. Engagement and level of thinking of both the students and the teachers have escaped from the boundaries of the "thinking boxes" that occur by relying on language only. Outside these confines, they have found a multiliterate, multimodal landscape of profoundly authentic talk. Here, students naturally make connections across texts and participate in roles and instructional practices that support high levels of thought.

Appendix A
Chapter Summaries

CHAPTER 1: ESSENTIAL COMPONENTS AND FRAMEWORKS

The visual of the multimedia text sets (MTS) framework (see figure 1.1, page 9) illustrates (1) a structure for balanced text selection, (2) the literacy practices that support learners, and (3) the instructional dispositions that provide a focus for planning, lesson development, and implementation.

Text Selection

To provide rich, accessible, engaging texts with the potential for layered meanings that spiral into deeper questioning and response, we provided a planning tool for text selection based on semiotic systems (Kress 2003):

- Linguistic (oral/written language)
- Visual (still/moving images)
- Auditory (music/sound)
- Gestural (facial expression/body language)
- Spatial (layout/organization of objects in space)

Literacy Practices

To plan for student engagement that supports a range of literacy practices and roles, we included the Four Resources Model proposed by Luke and Freebody (1999):

- Code breaker (coding competence)
- Meaning maker (semantic competence)
- Text user (pragmatic competence)
- Text critic (critical competence)

Connections: Text Selection and Literacy Practices

To illustrate how these literacy practices are used, we (1) presented a set of questions for each role that describe the role, (2) provided guiding questions that put each role into practice, (3) illustrated specific scaffolds that describe what elements of literacy are practiced in each role, and (4) described each role with specific examples.

Instructional Dispositions

As we designed the MTS framework, we identified six focal areas that incorporate instructional dispositions. We believe these instructional dispositions need to be present to meet the needs of adolescents. The dispositions are

- Writing practices (interweaving a variety of writing experiences, methods, and genres)
- Discussion across texts (collaboratively constructing meaning and sharing responses, viewpoints, and opinions of others)
- Vocabulary (understanding of and accurate use of words and concepts in a particular content area)
- Intertextual connections (texts are bound together by a set of relationships to other texts, beliefs, and values)
- Engagement (invested in and motivated to use background knowledge to construct and extend meanings through reading, writing, and discussion)
- Reading practices (engage in reading practices that include breaking the code, reading for different meanings, and understanding the uses and purposes of a range of texts)

Connections: Literacy Practices and Instructional Dispositions

Within each focal area, we provided a description of how these focal areas intersect and can be used to support the literacy practices of code breaker, meaning maker, text user, and text critic.

Writing Practices

- Writer as code breaker: Uses grammar, paragraph structure, and word choice that focus on organization.
- Writer as meaning maker: Understands and composes meaningful texts for particular audiences.
- Writer as text user: Understands and composes writing for different purposes.
- Writer as text critic: Understands how to shape writing by choosing different alternatives to fit different social and academic conditions.

Discussion Across Texts

- Discussion as code breaker: Recognizes the patterns and conventions, using language to articulate the differences within and between different forms of text.
- Discussion as meaning maker: Participates in meaning-making across text types, topics, or themes and verbally shares ideas, relationships, and experiences related to the texts.

- Discussion as text user: Verbally articulates different purposes and uses of particular kinds of text.

- Discussion as text critic: Responds, argues, and considers opposing viewpoints, using the vocabulary of text deconstruction.

Vocabulary

- Vocabulary as code breaker: Decodes language accurately within a particular context, content area, or situation.

- Vocabulary as meaning maker: Recognizes the variations in meanings and relationships of vocabulary across contexts.

- Vocabulary as text user: Uses background knowledge of vocabulary and of how language works to support understanding of content.

- Vocabulary as text critic: Analyzes the ways vocabulary is used to influence readers, listeners, and viewers.

In Stephanie's classroom:

In a lesson in the Americana unit, kinesthetic learning styles and musical intelligence were incorporated into vocabulary instruction using a modification of Beers' Idea Exchange (2003, 15), where the use of music, movement, writing, and talk focuses on words from various texts. In this MTS on the theme of Americana, students chose vocabulary from their self-selected texts to share with classmates. Words and meanings were shared and written. After several exchanges, the class came together to nominate great ideas heard during the exchange. Beers suggests that asking students to choose what they consider the most important words from their reading encourages a lively debate across students and texts. It also compels students to reread and to consider what is important for others to know.

Intertextual Connections

- Intertextuality as code breaker: Recognizes the patterns and conventions across text forms and how they create similar or different meanings in different contexts.

- Intertextuality as meaning maker: Is aware of how ideas are put together through comparison of different meanings of the same content across texts.

- Intertextuality as text user: Understands how ideas about the same content across different texts are put together and used.

- Intertextuality as text critic: Compares how texts each represent a perspective that attempts to influence some ideas while silencing others.

In Holly's classroom:

When her students read F. Scott Fitzgerald's *The Great Gatsby*, Holly added essays on the American Dream for them to read and asked students, "How is Gatsby a reflection of the American Dream?" Pairing related texts promoted connections that enabled students to think more critically about the American Dream and the theme of the novel.

Engagement

- Engagement as code breaker: Participates in making sense of and closely examining a range of familiar and unfamiliar texts.

- Engagement as meaning maker: Participates in meaning making of texts by using background knowledge and interests to make personal connections and find significance in texts.

- Engagement as text user: Uses knowledge of the world and other text forms to understand the uses of texts in different contexts.

- Engagement as text critic: Engages in analyzing the ways in which text is used to influence through critique, response, and taking a stance.

Reading Practices

- Reading practices as code breaker: Continuously breaks the code of all types of texts.

- Reading practices as meaning maker: Uses meaning-making tools (like graphic organizers) to support construction of meaning across text types, genres, and codes.

- Reading practices as text user: Uses the language structure and tone in texts to understand how to use the texts for different purposes that might persuade or influence the reader.

- Reading practices as text critic: Analyzes and second guesses texts through critical questions that consider different meanings and perspectives.

CHAPTER 2: ATHLETE AS CODE BREAKER

The code breaker recognizes and uses the structural conventions and patterns in all text types. Like an athlete, students in this role practice the patterns and conventions together and learn how to work together as a team to bring about the results they seek. Also, like an athlete who breaks down plays to study them, the code breaker prepares to read a text by breaking down its elements, organizing them, and examining how each element interacts as a whole.

Code Breaker in Stephanie's Americana Unit

Sequence: Brainstorm different text forms that communicate, unpack decisions of author/creator of text, practice being official code breaker, write the steps as the teacher models the role, work in pairs to break the code of different text types so that they can "teach" their classmates how to read their text.

Result: Students learned how to approach and deconstruct a wide range of texts in different situations. They discovered how practice and experience can lead to winning the code-breaking game.

Code Breaker in Holly's American Dream Unit

Sequence: Read background and history, work on anticipation guide, analyze photographs, analyze Fitzgerald quote, examine ideas graphic organizer introduces and adds, read/deconstruct novel in threaded Internet discussion, deconstruct and analyze film clips, compare text forms, and analyze director's/author's texts.

Result: Students learned how to code break visual and print texts. Like athletes, they used their skills (vocabulary, organization, and characterization strategies) to elevate their level of play.

Code Breaker in Richard's Vietnam War Unit

Sequence: Use graphic organizer to consider essential questions, play the code-breaking game by responding to anticipation guide, discuss possible game plans for reading texts, use code-breaking strategies to discuss texts, and return to game plan to analyze effectiveness.

Result: Students were coached as they broke the code of various text forms with conflicting perspectives. The students used vocabulary, prior knowledge, visual cues, and discussion to break the code and uncover the game plan embedded in each text form.

CHAPTER 3: ARCHAEOLOGIST AS MEANING MAKER

Meaning is constructed by reading and analyzing text, using knowledge of text conventions, purpose, and context. Like an archaeologist analyzing artifacts, the meaning maker tries to understand and compose texts based on concrete evidence and then think about the text as a social and cultural artifact. Also like an archaeologist, the students make meaning by gathering evidence and then studying the internal structures (text conventions), content, and contexts.

Meaning Maker in Stephanie's Americana Unit

Sequence: Reflect on code-breaker role, brainstorm, practice meaning making, observe teacher modeling explanation of one text moment, make meaning by making connections and presenting new ideas and meaningful quotes, define Americana.

Result: Students learned how to construct meaning by digging more deeply into the meaning behind the words. They developed voice, opinion, and point of view by actively participating in writing and articulating meaning.

Meaning Maker in Holly's American Dream Unit

Sequence: Build predictions, assemble characters' profiles through character quotes, identify trait descriptors to match quotes, compare with other students' descriptors, track a main character, and work in small groups to produce a body biography of the character.

Result: Students learned how to uncover and make meaning from cultural artifacts (text, dialogue, film, art).

Meaning Maker in Richard's Vietnam War Unit

Sequence: Activate prior knowledge, present the archaeologist metaphor, develop a stance toward the artifacts used, recognize patterns and unfamiliar meanings, raise questions, use graphic organizer to identify and synthesize new ideas.

Result: A wide range of experiences were modeled and used to make meaning from gathered artifacts – *New York Times* article, *60 Minutes* video, short fiction and nonfiction selections, music, photographs, and graphic organizers. This prompted students to unearth new meanings and perspectives by gathering evidence from a mixture of different text styles.

In Richard's classroom:

As Richard's students used a graphic organizer and questioning strategies to deconstruct and analyze Joe Sacco's (2001) political cartoon, they were explicitly taught how to break the code of this text and then consider multiple meanings during classroom discussion. Next, students looked at how this text, created about 30 years after the actual event, might reflect a different perspective. Students also looked carefully at Sacco, the political satirist who authored the cartoon, and asked which positions were present and absent in the text he created.

Students did not know, for instance, that Bob Kerrey's decision was at least partially based on the United States' "Rules of Engagement," a set of rules each soldier and leader is required to follow. When the text "Rules of Engagement" was introduced, this altered their understanding of both texts and added to their ability to analyze the event. In MTS, students use their prior knowledge but also build their prior knowledge as they work through the text set.

Thus, when students compared the political cartoon text to the cover photograph and printed text of the *New York Times Magazine* article about Bob Kerrey, they were able to read and deconstruct each text and then make intertextual connections by comparing the content, context, and purpose of each text.

CHAPTER 4: TOUR GUIDE AS TEXT USER

The text user recognizes the influence of text and understands the purposes and audiences for different forms of text. Texts are used in different ways for different purposes. Like a tour guide, the text user recognizes the text as a social and cultural artifact and composes texts that communicate particular meanings successfully. Also like a tour guide, students use prior knowledge and understanding of content and context to guide themselves in recognizing the purpose of text, authorial intent, and cultural motivation.

Text User in Stephanie's Americana Unit

Sequence: Survey image-based texts and note what is pictured and what is not pictured, analyze and infer author's message, verbally discuss and present ideas to classmates, apply knowledge, and lead the class on tours of how to read their visual texts.

Result: Students learned how to approach and deconstruct visual texts, articulated their thinking with writing, and guided others to comprehend inferential meanings.

Text User in Holly's American Dream Unit

Sequence: Connect and compare ideas from multiple texts, use academic talk, analyze contemporary film and add to graphic organizer, present and support information through interview/interviewee roles.

Result: Students learned character analysis using visual and print texts. They took a guided tour through multiple texts and traveled the same paths as the characters in the multimedia text sets.

Text User in Richard's Vietnam War Unit

Sequence: Activate prior knowledge, use highlighters and sticky notes while reading a challenging article, complete a graphic organizer to visually differentiate perspectives, view news-based TV clip and add to organizer, deliberate over perspectives from multiple text forms.

Result: Students practiced reading diverse print and video texts. Students toured different contexts of experience and began to articulate their connections and understandings of authorial intent while using the vocabulary of the content.

CHAPTER 5: FILM REVIEWER AS TEXT CRITIC

The text critic recognizes that texts have multiple points of view that influence and silence particular audiences, and critiques the embedded messages within different text forms. Like a film reviewer, the text critic has deep understanding of content, context, and audience and has the ability to analyze the meaning of texts by critiquing different points of view. Also like a film reviewer, students in this role critically analyze texts, articulate their understandings, and challenge the way the texts are constructed.

Text Critic in Stephanie's Americana Unit

Sequence: Introduce role of text critic, survey examples of film reviews and develop a guide that includes questions to help students think like a film critic, compile completed guides and develop a class guide, read and rate books for "Best Americana

Text," use the guides to critique recommended texts, engage in panel discussions, and vote to determine best text.

Result: Students learned how to use questioning effectively in their role as critic. They articulated their thinking with writing, and applied their knowledge by taking on the role of reviewer and text critic.

In Stephanie's classroom:

The students discussed the perspective of Hampton Sides in his book *Americana* (2004). The whole class engaged in discussion as text critic as they responded to Sides' perspective of "American-ness." As students shared their own written personal perceptions of American culture with their peers, they engaged in discussion as meaning makers by making connections across Sides' text, student-generated texts, verbally shared ideas, relationships, and experiences.

Text Critic in Holly's American Dream Unit

Sequence: Compare ideas from two articles about *The Great Gatsby*; use code breaking to identify assertions and evidence; use technology for written response; articulate their opinions of the American Dream, Fitzgerald, and universal themes.

Result: Students drew on all selections in their multimedia text sets to formulate their own American Dreams. Like film reviewers, they analyzed and considered the various perspectives from all the texts, used blogging to debate and question, and formed their own beliefs.

Text Critic in Richard's Vietnam War Unit

Sequence: Introduce the role of text critic, draw upon all four literacy practices (code breaker, meaning maker, text user, text critic) to develop an original poem synthesized from the ideas and content of the unit's multimedia text sets and subsequent research.

Result: Students combined resources and knowledge to examine texts to form inferences, to speculate, and to create meaning. A new text was developed that articulated the opinions and multiple perspectives in relationship to the essential questions driving this unit.

In Richard's classroom:

As code breakers, students deconstructed a political cartoon. They then moved to meaning making as they considered the meaning of the visual and print elements. As students constructed and performed their poems for multiple voices, discussions moved to the usefulness of structuring their poems and performance in particular ways. They practiced being text critics as they critiqued one another's poem and performance.

Appendix B
Reproducible Masters

Role [description]	Practices [questions]	Scaffolds [literacy]	MTS [context]
Code breaker (coding competence): breaks code of all texts (print, visual, multimodal) going beyond decoding to recognizing and using structural conventions and patterns	• How do I deconstruct this text? How does it work? • What are its patterns and conventions? • How do the sounds and the marks relate, singly, and in combination?	Students are taught to identify and use semiotic systems* to "make sense of marks on the page…gestures…tone" (Anstey and Bull 2006, 44) in order to figure out how texts work.	
Meaning maker (semantic competence): takes part in understanding and composing all texts based on prior knowledge and experiences of other cultural discourses, texts, and meaning systems	• How do the ideas represented in the text string together? • What cultural resources can be used to make meaning? • What are the cultural meanings and possible readings?	Students are taught to bring their schemata and prior knowledge (based on culture, community, and gender) to texts; they also need to be taught to recognize and compare those to different genres, text structures, and schemata in new contexts.	
Text user (pragmatic competence): knows about and acts on the different cultural and social functions of various texts in and out of school (functions shape text structure, tone, purpose, organization)	• How do the users of this text shape its composition? • What do I do with this text, here and now? • What will others do with it? • What are my options and alternatives?	Students are taught to understand that texts are always situated in fields of economic, cultural, and social fields of power. Students are also taught to read contexts of everyday use – to assess how technical features are used in different contexts and power structures.	
Text critic (critical competence): analyzes and changes meaning of texts by acting on the understanding and critiquing different points of view that can silence and influence	• What kind of person with what interests and values, could both write and read this naively and unproblematically? • What is this text trying to do to me? In whose interests? • Which positions, voices, and interests are at play? Which are silent and absent?	Students are taught to second guess the conditions of text production and text reception. Students are also taught to consider preferred and oppositional readings and how texts are constructed and produced to bring about particular responses.	

BLM 1: Literacy practices chart

Adapted from Luke 2000; Anstey and Bull 2006; Luke and Freebody 1999. ©Portage & Main Press, 2010, *Multimedia Text Sets,* ISBN: 978-1-55379-248-2

Lesson Aims	Lesson Sequence Details
I want my students to:	

© Portage & Main Press, 2010, *Multimedia Text Sets*, ISBN: 978-1-55379-248-2

BLM 2: Lesson plan chart

Text Type	Linguistic (oral/written language)	Visual (still/moving images)	Auditory (music/sound)	Gestural (facial expression/body language)	Spatial (layout/organization of objects in space)

BLM 3: Text-selection chart

Adapted from Anstey and Bull 2006. © Portage & Main Press, 2010, *Multimedia Text Sets*, ISBN: 978-1-55379-248-2

Text Type	Semiotic System	Genre	Learning Purpose	What Students Need to Know	What Students Need to Be Able to Do

Adapted from Anstey and Bull 2006. © Portage & Main Press, 2010, *Multimedia Text Sets*, ISBN: 978-1-55379-248-2

BLM 4: Text analysis chart

Body Biography

For your chosen or appointed character, you will create a body biography – a visual and written portrait illustrating several aspects of your character's life within the novel.

You have many possibilities for filling up your poster paper or screen (check templates in the computer program you are using, for example). Several choices are listed below; feel free to come up with your own creations and ideas. The choices you make should be based on the text – but also exhibit creativity and analysis.

Your portrait *must* include the following:

❑ A review of significant happenings in the novel

❑ Visual symbols and expansion vocabulary

❑ Some representation of your character that relates to the theme of this unit

❑ A portion of the original text

❑ Your character's *three* most important lines from the story (make sure the lines are not from the portion of the original text you have already used)

Suggestions:

- Placement: Carefully choose the placement of your text and artwork. For example, the area where your character's heart would be might be appropriate for illustrating the important relationships within his or her life.

- Spine: Actors often discuss a character's spine. What is your character's most important goal? What drives his or her thoughts and actions? This is his or her spine. How can you symbolize or illustrate it?

- Virtues and vices (vocabulary component): In *sophisticated expansion vocabulary*, what are your character's most admirable qualities? His or her worst characteristics? How can you make us visualize them?

- Color: Colors are often symbolic, and many stories are heavy with color symbolism. What color(s) do you most associate with your character? Why? How can you effectively work these colors into your presentation? Here are a list of colors and the traditional symbolic associations that Western culture attributes to each:

    White: purity, innocence, cleanliness, heaven, Caucasians

    Yellow: aging, decaying, sunshine, warmth

    Blue: sadness, depression, cold

    Silver: wealth, decadence

    Green: youth, newness, inexperience, seasickness, envy

- Symbols: What objects can you associate with your character that illustrate his or her essence? Are there objects mentioned within the novel itself that you could use (e.g., someone is "an absolute rose," "a gem," a work horse")? If not, choose objects that seem to signify an important aspect of that character.

- Mirror, mirror…: Consider both how your character appears to others on the surface and what you know about the character's inner self and moral stance. Do these images clash or correspond? What does this tell you about the character?

- Changes: How has your character changed (thinking, morals, actions, etc.) during the novel? Trace these changes in your text and/or artwork.

BLM 5: Body biography handout

Adapted from Smagorinsky and O'Donnell-Allen 1998. © Portage & Main Press, 2010, *Multimedia Text Sets*, ISBN: 978-1-55379-248-2

	Points Possible	Criteria for Earning the Highest Number of Points Possible	Points Earned
Review of Events	0–4	• The significant happenings relevant to your character are reviewed (displayed) visually.	
Visual Elements	0–12	• Visual symbols show a strong connection to the essence of your character. • Symbols are clearly connected to the text. • Colors used are symbolic. • Character's most/least admirable qualities are illustrated visually and are represented by expansion vocabulary. • Inner struggle or goal of your character is illustrated. • Symbols and texts display important relationships or issues in your character's life.	
Original Text	0–4	• A carefully selected, pivotal portion of the original text is included.	
Character Dialogue	0–4	• Your character's three most pivotal lines (not from the same passage, page, or chapter) are on the body biography.	
Character Analysis	0–4	• Images in the visual illustrate how the character appears to others and also display the character's inner self. • Significant character changes are illustrated.	
Written Explanation	0–12	• Explained how and why you chose to use the visual elements and provided text evidence to account for what they reveal about your character • Explained your reason for choosing the pivotal segment of original text • Explained how the character's dialogue reveals something significant about him/her • Explained the ways in which the visuals show how the character appears to others, while also revealing the character's inner self, morals • Explained how the body biography illustrates character changes	40 Pt. Total

BLM 6: Rubric for body biography

Adapted from Smagorinsky and O'Donnell-Allen 1998. © Portage & Main Press, 2010, *Multimedia Text Sets*, ISBN: 978-1-55379-248-2

Photograph #: _____

What do you see? List everything.	What do you think the photograph means?
	Positive or negative feelings toward the subject?

Do you get a sense of the photographer's message? What is the photographer's point of view?

_____

What do you think is the connecting theme between the photographs?

_____

What is the author's overall purpose?

_____

Photograph #: _____

What do you see? List everything.	What do you think the photograph means?
	Positive or negative feelings toward the subject?

Do you get a sense of the photographer's message? What is the photographer's point of view?

_____

What do you think is the connecting theme between the photographs?

_____

What is the author's overall purpose?

_____

BLM 7: Reading photographs

©Portage & Main Press, 2010, *Multimedia Text Sets*, ISBN: 978-1-55379-248-2

PANEL INTERVIEW WITH HOTSEATING: A PLANNING GUIDE

Your body biography character from novel being studied:

_____

Your assigned character(s) from a YA novel:

_____

Assigned "Land" for your panel interview:

_____

Assignment

Your job: Role-play your assigned characters and reflect your understanding of the theme in _____ .

_____ and in one of the three following novels:

_____

_____

> Note: If a question is posed to you that cannot be answered with direct evidence from the novels, you will have to "infer" or make an educated guess about it.

> Note: Assume that all panelists know the stories of the others, including those from other novels.

Your assessment: The panel interview is worth 30 points, and the individual written portion worth 10 points. The written individual portion will be an assessment of the panel experience and your contributions to it.

How to prepare: Convene with your character groups, and generate responses to these aspects of your character. Tap into your body biographies and the two novels you have read to generate well-rounded perspectives. Remember that you can portray your characters through quotes from other characters (especially if your character does not appear in every chapter).

1. List your passions, deepest desires (which may not be mentioned in the text), and what you symbolize or stand for. Provide evidence from the two novels.

    (a) Character from novel 1:

    _____

    _____

    _____

    _____

    (b) Character from novel 2:

    _____

    _____

    _____

    _____

2. List your main dreams and goals in life. Provide evidence from the two novels.

    (a) Character from novel 1:

    _____

    _____

    _____

    _____

©Portage & Main Press, 2010, *Multimedia Text Sets*, ISBN: 978-1-55379-248-

(b) Character from novel 2:

_____

_____

_____

3. What are your biggest obstacles and problems? Provide evidence from the two novels.
    (a) Character from novel 1:

_____

_____

_____

_____

    (b) Character from novel 2:

_____

_____

_____

_____

4. List your greatest strengths and weaknesses. Provide evidence from the two novels.
    (a) Character from novel 1:

_____

_____

_____

_____

    (b) Character from novel 2:

_____

_____

_____

_____

5. Use sophisticated (expansion) vocabulary to describe your character. Provide evidence from the two novels:
    (a) Character from novel 1:

_____

_____

_____

_____

    (b) Character from novel 2:

_____

_____

_____

_____

BLM 8: (cont'd)

©Portage & Main Press, 2010, *Multimedia Text Sets*, ISBN: 978-1-55379-248-2

Page	Details
Front cover	Create a symbolic front cover for your book that brings together all of the most important aspects of your book – characters, themes, words, events. It should NOT be a picture of a scene from a book – too easy!
1	Detailed explanation of front cover: What did you include? Why did you include them? Write in sentences and paragraphs.
2	**At least 3** text-to-text connections: Does your text remind you of any other text? Remember a text can be anything that communicates a message – a novel, a poem, a photograph, a song, a film, a TV show, etc.
3	**At least 3** text-to-world connections: Does your text remind you of any current issues belonging to today's world? Does it remind you of anything that happened in the past.
4	**At least 3** text-to-country connections: Does the book remind you of people, places, events, beliefs, philosophies, attitudes that you have read about, seen, or experienced yourself?
5	**Author's purpose:** Why did the author write the book? Is there a message or moral for the reader? What is it? Think about major themes (e.g., love, hate, racism, supremacy, friendship, betrayal) – what does the author say about them? Explain and refer in detail to specific parts of the book to score top grades.
6	**Comment on book's audience:** What kind of person or audience was your text written for? How do you know? Do you fit into the intended audience? Did the intended audience of the text affect your enjoyment?
7	**Comment on audience reaction to book:** How did you react to the book and the things that happened in your text? Would other people with different lives, situations, and experiences react differently to your text? Be specific with your answers – talk to others if necessary.
8	**Evaluation:** What were the best things about your book? What could the author have done to improve or make it better?
Elective Pages	• Visualizations: images of characters, settings, maps, timelines, events, etc. • Quotation analysis: key words, phrases, and lines • Comprehension: character, setting, plot work (your choice) • Knowledge recall: interesting facts and details about people and places • Artistic: scrapbook pages, journal entries, letters, poetry, comic strip, etc. • Your choice: Anything else you can think of?

BLM 9: Mini-guide handout

©Portage & Main Press, 2010, *Multimedia Text Sets*, ISBN: 978-1-55379-248-2

Resources

REFERENCES

Allen, J. *Inside Words: Tools for Teaching Academic Vocabulary, Grades 4–12*. Portland, ME: Stenhouse, 2007.

Almasi, J. F. "The Nature of Fourth Graders' Sociocognitive Conflicts in Peer-Led and Teacher-Led Discussions of Literature." *Reading Research Quarterly* 30 (1995): 314–351.

Alvermann, D. E. "Effective Literacy Instruction for Adolescents." Executive Summary and Paper Commissioned by the National Reading Conference. Chicago, IL: National Reading Conference, 2001.

Alvermann, D. E., and A. J. Eakle. "Comprehension Instruction: Adolescents and Their Mulitple Literacies." In *Rethinking Reading Comprehension*, edited by A. P. Sweet and C. E. Snow. New York: Guilford, 2003.

Alvermann, D.E., and S. F. Phelps. *Content Reading and Literacy: Succeeding in Today's Diverse Classrooms*. 4th ed. Boston: Allyn and Bacon, 2004.

Alvermann, D. E., S. F. Phelps, and V. G. Ridgeway. *Content Reading and Literacy: Succeeding in Today's Diverse Classrooms*. 5th ed. Boston: Pearson, 2007.

Anstey, M., and G. Bull. *Teaching and Learning Multiliteracies: Changing Times, Changing Literacies*. Newark, DE: International Reading Association, 2006.

Armbruster, B., F. Lehr, and J. Osborn. Putting Reading First: The Research Building Blocks for Teaching Children to Read. Jessup, MD: National Institute for Literacy, 2001.

Armbruster, B. B., S. J. McCarthey, and S. Cummins. "Writing to Learn in Elementary Grades." In *Learning to Write, Writing to Learn: Theory and Research in Practice*, edited by R. Indrisano and J. R. Paratore. Newark, DE: International Reading Association, 2005.

Barthes, R. *Writing Degree Zero*. New York: Hill and Wang, 1967.

Bean, T. W. "Reading in the Content Areas: Social Constructivist Dimensions." In *Handbook of Reading Research, Volume III*, edited by M. L. Kamil, P. B. Mosenthal, P. D. Pearson, and R. Barr. Mahwah, NJ: Erlbaum, 2000.

Beers, K. *When Kids Can't Read – What Teachers Can Do: A Guide for Teachers 6–12*. Portsmouth, NH: Heinemann, 2003.

Behrman, E. H. "Teaching About Language, Power, and Text: A Review of Classroom Practices that Support Critical Literacy." *Journal of Adolescent & Adult Literacy* 49 (2006): 490–498.

Biancarosa, G., and C. Snow. *Reading Next – A Vision for Action and Research in Middle School and High School Literacy: A Report to Carnegie Corporation of New York*. Washington, DC: Alliance for Excellent Education, 2004.

Blachowicz, C. L. Z. "Making Connections: Alternatives to the Vocabulary Notebook." *Journal of Reading* 29 (1986): 643–649.

Bourdieu, P. *Practical Reason.* Cambridge, UK: Polity Press, 1998.

Brenner, D., P. D. Pearson, and L. Rief, "Thinking Through Assessment." In *Adolescent Literacy: Turning Promise into Practice*, edited by K. Beers, R. E. Probst, and L. Reif. Portsmouth, NH: Heinemann, 2007.

Britton, J., et al. *The Development of Writing Abilities*. London: Macmillan Education, 1975.

Bruner, J. *The Culture of Education*. Cambridge, MA: Harvard University Press, 1996.

Buehl, D. *Classroom Strategies for Interactive Learning*. 2nd ed. Newark, DE: International Reading Association, 2001.

Burke, J. "Teaching English Language Arts in a 'Flat' World." In *Adolescent Literacy: Turning Promise into Practice*, edited by K. Beers, R. E. Probst, and L. Reif. Portsmouth, NH: Heinemann, 2007.

Calkins, L. *The Art of Teaching Writing*. Toronto: Irwin Publishing, 1994.

Ebert, R. "The City of Ember." *Chicago Sun-Times* (8 October 2008).

_____. "The Secret Life of Bees." *Chicago Sun-Times* (15 October 2008).

Fleischman, P. *Joyful Noise: Poems for Two Voices*. New York: HarperCollins, 1989.

Fletcher, R. *A Writer's Notebook: Unlocking the Writer Within You*. New York: Avon-Camelot, 1997.

Fulwiler, T., and A. Young. *Connections: Writing and Reading Across the Curriculum*. Urbana, IL: NCTE, 1982.

Galda, L., and M. F. Graves. *Reading and Responding in the Middle Grades: Approaches for All Classrooms*. Boston: Pearson, 2007.

Gall, M. D., and J. P. Gall. "Teacher and Student Roles in Different Types of Classroom Discussions." (ERIC Document Reproduction Services No. ED 359 256), 1993.

Gallagher, K. *Deeper Reading: Comprehending Challenging Texts, 4–12.* Portland, ME: Stenhouse, 2004.

_____. *Reading Reasons: Motivational Mini-Lessons for Middle and High School*. Portland, ME: Stenhouse, 2003.

Gambrell, L. B., and J. F. Almasi. *Lively Discussions!: Fostering Engaged Reading*. Newark, DE: International Reading Association, 1996.

Gammill, D. M. "Learning the Write Way." *The Reading Teacher* 59: 8 (May 2006): 754–762.

Gee, J. P. *Situated Language and Learning: A Critique of Traditional Schooling*. New York: Routledge, 2004.

_____. *An Introduction to Discourse Analysis: Theory and Method*. London: Routledge, 1999.

_____. *Social Linguistics and Literacies: Ideology in Discourses*. Bristol, PA: Taylor and Francis, 1996.

Guthrie, J. T., and S. Ozgungor. "Instructional Contexts for Reading Engagement." In *Comprehension Instruction: Research-Based Best Practices*, edited by C. C. Block and M. Pressley. New York: Guilford, 2002.

Hern, L. C., M. Faust, and M. Boyd. "Literacy, Textuality, and the Expert: Learning in the English Language Arts." In *Learning from Text Across Conceptual Domains*, edited by C. R. Hynd. Mahwah, NJ: Lawrence Erlbaum Associates, 1998.

Hynd, C. R., and S. A. Stahl. "What Do We Mean by Knowledge and Learning?" In *Learning From Text Across Conceptual Domains*, edited by C. R. Hynd. Mahwah, NJ: Lawrence Erlbaum Associates, 1998.

Irvin, J. L., et al. *Strategies to Enhance Literacy and Learning in Middle School Content Area Classrooms*. Boston: Pearson/Allyn and Bacon, 2007.

Jeffrey, N., and B. Prentice. *Writing in the Middle and Secondary Classrooms*. Toronto: ITP Nelson, 1997.

Keene, E. O., and S. Zimmermann. *Mosaic of Thought: The Power of Comprehension Strategy Instruction*. Portsmouth, NH: Heinemann, 2007.

Ketch, A. "Conversation: The Comprehension Connection." *The Reading Teacher* 59:1 (2005): 8.

King-Shaver, B. *When Texts Meets Text: Helping High School Readers Make Connections in Literature*. Portsmouth, NH: Heinemann, 2005.

Kress, G. *Literacy in the New Media Age*. New York: Routledge, 2003.

Langer, J. *Effective Literacy Instruction: Building Successful Reading and Writing Programs*. Urbana, IL: NCTE, 2002.

Luke, A. "Critical Literacy in Australia: A Matter of Context and Standpoint." *Journal of Adolescent & Adult Literacy* 43 (2000): 448–461.

Luke, A., and P. Freebody. "Further Notes on the Four Resources Model." 1999, http://www.readingonline.org/research/lukefreebody.html (retrieved January 22, 2008).

Moon, B. *Literary Terms: A Practical Glossary*. Urbana, IL: National Council of Teachers of English, 1999.

National Park Service: U.S. Department of the Interior. http://www.nps.gov/history/archeology/AforI/whisar_intr.htm (retrieved July 28, 2008).

Ogle, D., and C. L. Z. Blachowicz. "Beyond Literature Circles: Helping Students Comprehend Informational Texts." In *Comprehension Instruction: Research-Based Best Practices*, edited by C. C. Block and M. Pressley. New York: Guilford, 2002.

Paterson, K. *A Sense of Wonder: On Reading and Writing Books for Children*. New York: Plume, 1995.

Pressley, M. "What Should Comprehension Instruction Be the Instruction Of?" In *Handbook of Reading Research, Vol. III*, edited by M. L. Kamil, P. D. Pearson, and R. Barr. Mahwah, NJ: Erlbaum, 2000.

Reinking, D., and D. Leu. "Understanding Internet Reading Comprehension and its Development Among Adolescents at Risk of Dropping Out of School." Report of work on the TICA Project at the National Reading Conference, Austin, TX, November 30, 2007.

Rosenblatt, L. *Literature as Exploration*. New York: Noble and Noble, 1968.

Santman, D. *Shades of Meaning: Comprehension and Interpretation in Middle School*. Portsmouth, NH: Heinemann, 2005.

Scarborough, H. S., "Connecting Early Language and Literacy to Later Reading (Dis)abilities: Evidence, Theory, and Practice." In *Handbook of Early Literacy Research,* 97–110, edited by S. B. Neuman and D. K. Dickinson. New York: Guilford, 2001.

Smagorinsky, P., and C. O'Donnell-Allen. "Reading as Mediated and Mediating Action: Composing Meaning for Literature Through Multimedia Interpretive Texts." *Reading Research Quarterly* 33, 2 (April/May/June 1998): 198–226.

Snow, C. E., P. Griffin, and M. S. Burns. *Knowledge to Support the Teaching of Reading: Preparing Teachers for a Changing World.* San Francisco: Jossey-Bass, 2005.

Snow, C. E., and A. P. Sweet. "Reading for Comprehension." In *Rethinking Reading Comprehension,* edited by A. P. Sweet and C. E. Snow. New York: Guilford, 2003.

Sullivan, S. "Introduction: Media Literacy: Finding a Foothold in the English Classroom." In *Lesson Plans for Creating Media-Rich Classrooms,* edited by M. T. Christel and S. Sullivan. Urbana, IL: National Council of Teachers of English, 2007.

Thompson, A. "Eternally Modern: Fitzgerald Connects Jazz Age to Generation X." *Wisconsin State Journal* (10 September 1996).

Tomlinson, C., and J. McTighe. *Integrating Differentiated Instruction and Understanding by Design: Connecting Content and Kids.* Alexandria, VA: ASCD, 2006.

Tovani, C. *I Read It, But I Don't Get It.* New York: Stenhouse, 2000.

Vacca, J. L., R. T. Vacca, and M. K. Gove. *Reading and Learning to Read.* 4th ed. New York: Longman, 2000.

Vygotsky, L. M. *Mind in Society: The Development of Higher Psychological Processes.* Cambridge, MA: Harvard University Press, 1978.

Wade, S. W., and E. B. Moje. "The Role of Text in Classroom Learning." In *Handbook of Reading Research, Volume III,* edited by M. L. Kamil, P. B. Mosenthal, P. D. Pearson, and R. Barr. Mahwah, NJ: Erlbaum, 2000.

Wilhelm, J. D. *Engaging Readers and Writers with Inquiry.* New York: Scholastic, 2007.

————. *You Gotta Be the Book: Teaching Engaged and Reflective Reading with Adolescents.* New York: Teachers College Press, 1997.

Wilhelm, J. D., and M. W. Smith. "Making it Matter Through the Power of Inquiry." In *Adolescent Literacy: Turning Promise into Practice,* edited by K. Beers, R. E. Probst, and L. Reif. Portsmouth, NH: Heinemann, 2007.

RESOURCES CITED

Print

Alexie, S. *The Absolutely True Diary of a Part-Time Indian*. New York: Little Brown, 2007.

Coy, J. *Crackback*. New York: Scholastic, 2005.

Fleischman, P. *Joyful Noise: Poems for Two Voices*. New York: HarperCollins, 1988.

Fitzgerald, F. S. *The Great Gatsby*. New York: Charles Scribner's Sons, 1925.

_____. *This Side of Paradise*. New York: Classic Books International, 2009 (originally published 1920).

Harrison, L. The Clique series. New York: Poppy; Little, Brown, 2008.

Hesse, K. *Out of the Dust*. New York: Scholastic, 1997.

Hinton, S. E. *The Outsiders*. New York: Viking Press, 1967.

Jenkins, P. *A Walk Across America*. New York: Morrow, 1979.

Johnston, T. *Bone by Bone by Bone*. New Milford, CT: Roaring Brook Press, 2007.

Knight. M. B., and A. S. O'Brien. *Talking Walls*. Gardiner, ME: Tilbury House, 1995.

Lyons, L. *Flag: An American Story*. London, UK: Vision on Publishing, 2001.

Myers, W. D. *Monster*. New York: Amistad, 1999.

Na, A. *Wait for Me*. New York: Putnam Juvenile (Penguin), 2006.

Philbrick, N. *Revenge of the Whale: The True Story of the Whaleship* Essex. New York: G. P. Putnam, 2002.

Portillo, E. "Village." In *Times of Changes: Vietnam and the 60s,* 56–63. Edited by S. V. Matthews. Des Moines, IA: Perfection Learning, 2001,

Rimer, S. "Teens Connect to Jay Gatsby and His Dream." *The New York Times* (17 February 2008).

Schlosser, E., and C. Wilson. *Chew on This: Everything You Don't Want to Know About Fast Food*. Boston: Houghton Mifflin, 2006.

Selznick, B. *The Invention of Hugo Cabret*. New York: Scholastic, 2007.

Sides, H. *Americana: Dispatches from the New Frontier*. Maine: Anchor, 2004.

Thompson, A. "Eternally Modern: Fitzgerald Connects Jazz Age to Generation X." *Wisconsin State Journal* (10 September 1996).

Thompson, H. "The Massacre at My Lai." In *Times of Change: Vietnam and the 60s,* 64–65. Edited by S. V. Matthews. Des Moine, IA: Perfection Learning, 2001.

Twain, M. *The Adventures of Huckleberry Finn*. New York: Charles L. Webster and Company, 1884.

Vistica, G. L. "One Awful Night in Thanh Phong." *The New York Times Magazine* (29 April 2001): 50–57, 66–68, 133.

Zusak, M. *Getting the Girl*. New York: Scholastic, 2003.

Video

Rather, D. "Memories of a Massacre." *CBS: 60 Minutes II*. Narrated by D. Rather. Produced by T. Anderson and G. Vistica. New York: CBS, 1 May 2001.

Film

G. Directed by Christopher Scott Cherot. Andrew Lauren Productions, New York, 2005 (DVD, 2006).

The City of Ember. Directed by Gil Kenan. 20th Century Fox, Los Angeles, 2008 (DVD, 2009).

The Great Gatsby. Directed by Jack Clayton. Paramount Pictures, Los Angeles, 1974 (DVD, 2006).

The Namesake. Directed by Mira Nair. Fox Searchlight, Los Angeles, 2007 (DVD, 2007).

The Secret Life of Bees. Directed by Gina Prince-Bythewood. 20th Century Fox, Los Angeles, 2008 (DVD, 2009).

Audio

Cohen, L. *Essential Leonard Cohen*. Anthem, 2008.

Moore, R., and B. Sadler. *Ballad of the Green Beret*, Barry Sadler, RCA Victor, 1966.

Websites

Writing Next:
http://www.all4ed.org/files/archive/publications/WritingNext/WritingNext.pdf

National Park Services, U.S. Department of the Interior:
http://www.nps.gov/history/archeology/Aforl/whisar_intr.htm

SUGGESTED READING

Albers, P. *Finding the Artist Within: Creating and Reading Visual Texts in the English Language Arts Classroom*. Newark, DE: International Reading Association, 2007.

Alvermann, D. E., S.F. Phelps, and V. R. Gillis. *Content Reading and Literacy: Succeeding in Today's Diverse Classrooms*. 6th ed. Boston: Pearson/Allyn and Bacon, 2010.

Anderson, R. C., and P. Freebody. "Vocabulary Knowledge." In *Comprehension and Teaching: Research Reviews*, edited by J. T. Guthrie. Newark, DE: International Reading Association, 1981.

Beers, K., R. E. Probst, and L. Reif (eds.). *Adolescent Literacy: Turning Promise into Practice*. Portsmouth, NH: Heinemann, 2007.

Booth, D. *Reading Doesn't Matter Anymore…: Shattering the Myths of Literacy*. Markham, ON: Pembroke Publishers, 2006.

Boyer, T. L. "Writing to Learn in Social Studies." *The Social Studies*. July/August (2006): 158–160.

Christel, M. T., and S. Sullivan (eds.). *Lesson Plans for Creating Media-Rich Classrooms*. Urbana, IL: National Council of Teachers of English, 2007.

Clarke, L. W. "Discussing Shiloh: A Conversation Beyond the Book." *Journal of Adolescent & Adult Literacy* 51(2007): 2.

Deshler, D. D., et al. *Informed Choices for Struggling Adolescent Readers: A Research-Based Guide to Instructional Programs and Practices*. Newark, DE: International Reading Association, 2007.

Golden, J. *Reading in the Reel World: Teaching Documentaries and Other Nonfiction Texts*. Urbana, IL: National Council of Teachers of English, 2006.

_____. *Reading in the Dark: Using Film as a Tool in the English Classroom*. Urbana, IL: National Council of Teachers of English, 2001.

Graham, S., and D. Perin. *Writing Next: Effective Strategies to Improve Writing of Adolescents in Middle and High Schools*. New York: Carnegie, 2007. See also: Corporation.http://www.all4ed.org/files/archive/publications/WritingNext/WritingNext.pdf

Gunning, T. G. *Developing Higher-Level Literacy in All Students: Building Reading, Reasoning, and Responding*. Boston: Pearson, 2008.

Honig, B. *Teaching Our Children to Read: The Components of an Effective, Comprehensive Reading Program*. Thousand Oaks, CA: Corwin Press, 2001.

Kajder, S. B. "Unleashing Potential with Emerging Technologies." In *Adolescent Literacy: Turning Promise into Practice*, edited by K. Beers, R. E. Probst, and L. Reif. Portsmouth, NH: Heinemann, 2007.

Knipper, K. J., and T. J. Duggan. "Writing to Learn Across the Curriculum: Tools for Comprehension in Content Area Classes." *The Reading Teacher* 59:5 (February 2006): 462–470.

Kress, G., and T. van Leeuwen. *Reading Images: The Grammar of Visual Design*. New York: Routledge, 1998.

Pearson, P. D., B. M. Taylor, and A. Tam. "Epilogue: Effective Professional Development for Improving Literacy Instruction." In *Learning to Write, Writing to Learn: Theory and Research in Practice*, edited by R. Indrisano, and J. R. Paratore. Newark, DE: International Reading Association, 2005.

Romano, T. "Teaching Writing from the Inside." In *Adolescent Literacy: Turning Promise into Practice*, edited by K. Beers, R. E. Probst, and L. Reif. Portsmouth, NH: Heinemann, 2007.

Schroeder, K. "Raising Writing Skills." In *Education Digest* 72:4 (December 2006): 74–76.